I0133208

God's Glorious Green Mountain

The Demons Within!

By:

David Stanfield

After a lifetime of church and all I have been taught, this I now understand, "God truly hates religion"

A biography of the psychological and spiritual long term affects of legalistic and binding religious theology.

ISBN: 978-0-578-04327-2

Printed in the United States by Morris Publishing

3212 East Highway 30

Kearney, NE 68847

1-800-650-7888

Dedicated

I proudly dedicate this book to my Beautiful Alexandria, whom I will protect and cherish all the days of my life. May the God of Heaven spare you the influence that resides within our family lines. I will teach and instruct you in the true doctrine of Christ so that you may avoid the character twisting pitfalls that have been instilled within me by well meaning "Godly" men. Remember the words of the Apostle Paul "all things are legal for the Christian, not all things are good for the Christian"! Trust in no man or doctrine above God, search his word for the answers to your questions and remember Christ is always with you, may your life be long and prosperous and may we be together forever in the everlasting life to come. After Jesus I live only for you! Please always see your father as he aspired to be, not as he actually was.

Prelude

After an unimaginable war in heaven God gathered forth the remnant of his elect that were spoiled, one third of his elite angels had chosen a path contrary to his will. Instead of destroying them he would allow them to follow their misguided leader, Lucifer, the most perfect and beautiful angel God had ever created. Follow him into an epic battle of good verses evil, while the end is quite foretold and the battles predestined, none the less God had his reasons to prolong the inevitable end to this conflict.

A choice, all of creation must make a choice, God reasoned, if my elect could turn against me and attempt to overthrow me, all of creation must choose once and for all. I will test all of the souls I have created; I will end this insurrection with absolute certainty, insuring the seeds of discontent are forever abolished in heaven. I have predestined all for my glory, now lets see how many will choose their creator over the deceiver. I will purchase their sin with the blood of my Son, I will send my Holy Spirit to comfort them, and the very power of heaven will be available at their beckoning call. They will be subjected to Satan's lies and deceit, they will be subjected to the demons within, those voices and passions that attempt to direct their lives. They will be subjected to the imperfect doctrines of men, now, how will they choose?

Chapter One

In the Beginning!

My first real conscious thoughts that have been retained within my memory are from about my fifth year of life. Growing up in several small towns in Illinois and spending the summers with my grandparents Charley and Ellen. They were grand people and I loved them dearly, quite old fashioned and very strict. Ellen was a devout Pentecostal and Charley was the husband that she prayed for daily, after all Jesus said "there are no good men". The roots of my many demons can be traced back to my grandparent's house starting with the upbringing of my mother.

Jewell, my mother, the only daughter of four children was raised on a small farm with no electricity or running water. Their meager existence was carved from grandpa working the soil and raising farm animals supplying their most basic needs. Within this wholesome family the values were such, no drinking, no swearing, no lewd behavior, absolute respect to your parents. For the girl child, my mother, no pants or modern fashions, ankle length dresses were the only option for her attire. Sex was obviously on the forbidden vise list, not only for the teenage children but apparently for grandpa too, we would learn many years later.

From my understanding it was basically a happy and healthy environment physically, steeped in hard work and focused on survival, the emotional ramifications of the strict, religious environment were yet to be realized and would take decades to fully manifest their complete emotional contributions.

Grandpa Charley was a big man, strong as an ox with a good heart but a very stubborn personality. While he generally tolerated Grandma's religion and devotion to God he would seldom participate and quickly grow agitated when remarks or soul saving efforts were focused at him. The few times Charley would escort Ellen to church it was generally a back pew, a short nap and a quick exit. Grandma on the other hand was full of joy and peace, I truly believe Ellen Hunt loved everyone she ever had the complete joy to meet. The mother Teresa of Carlinville Illinois, Ellen's life would be a testament to kindness, love for all of mankind and complete devotion to her God. What a burden she must have carried believing the husband she loved and cared for, by his own stubborn refusal to accept Gods grace, would not accompany her to the next life. What a horrible burden Grandpa he must have carried, being denied the basic needs of the flesh, with exception of maybe four occasions.

The Pentecostal Faith

The strict Holiness or Pentecostal faith is quite unyielding and harsh, applying ridged consequences for daily sins and shortcomings. One may have salvation as long as one stays pure and sinless, but with the first sin a regiment of requesting forgiveness is required to purchase Gods wonderful gift back once more. A constant struggle, a constant attempt to be perfect in your daily activities; Always requiring a steady stream of prayers for forgiveness, please forgive me lord, please forgive me lord, dare not go to sleep and forget your prayers, what if you had sinned that day?

After all we were taught if you die in your sins you go to hell, regardless of your past confession of faith. It was so many years later I would realize for myself the folly in such beliefs and the permanent damage instilled within my person by the legalistic doctrines of well meaning men.

In fact the belief that one could control themselves with such conviction as to not sin, is entirely impossible. The belief that one could elevate one's flesh up to a sinless, holy nature by virtue of ones self control in fact would negate the need for Gods grace and salvation altogether.

An unyielding doctrine, conceived in the Old Covenant law given by God to Moses and intermingled with choice portions of the New Covenant Grace, given to all of mankind by Christ. This hybrid, harsh and strict Covenant, conceived and written by man would prove to be an unmovable rock that would crush the souls, including mine, that would fall against it.

My mother's teenage years were the toughest of all, a literal prisoner's life she would endure, while her brothers seemed to be given a little freedom, the female child must be preserved and protected from the world at all costs. Her days consisted of going to school and coming immediately home afterwards. Absolutely no extracurricular activities or after school friends were allowed, and don't even mention boys. My mother tells me stories of how she wasn't allowed to date, was only allowed to swim if she were wearing a floor length dress, no music or dancing, none of the common things associated with a young persons life were allowed.

At the first opportunity Jewell hurriedly married to escape the confinement and miserable existence of her parent's home. She would find out later that freedom is not always worth the price paid. Or with hind sight one type of confinement would be traded for another of equal torment.

How often do the overenthusiastic good intentions of parents destroy the abilities of children to grow and become well balanced persons? Wouldn't it be better and more beneficial to lengthen the ties as the child matures and proves their responsibility?

Robert was a thin lanky man of about 6' tall, slightly handsome and already chain smoking at 20 years of age. He would do, she thought, I have a good heart and I can love anyone, he will do. Over the protest of her parents Jewell and Robert were married. Freedom had come at last for this eighteen year old young woman eager to experience the simple pleasures of life. With hope and great anticipation of actually living and making choices for herself Jewell embarked on this journey called marriage.

Young people often dream of their wedding night and the incredible exhilaration of becoming intimate with another person for the first time. The most powerful and passionate expectations of humanity are associate with this time of life. Unfortunately when you wake up the next morning completely convinced that your going to hell for what you have done the night before, it tends to drench the passion and limit such future activities.

Strict religious indoctrination that ones body was not to be seen by anyone else, let alone enjoyed or touched would sound like a warning siren within her head. For the old church mother says that sex is to be tolerated only in the dark, and for the purpose of bearing children. Your body is Gods temple and dare no man defile Gods temple. The demons within would manifest and torment her for her horrible acts, the acts of a free woman, free to make choices free to live and to love and even experience physical love, and free to abandon those beliefs so strictly imposed on her life.

The sins of a Pentecostal are many, as my mother would soon realize, free now to wear shorts, swim suits and modern fashions. Free to listen to music, go dancing or stay out late, free to go anywhere she wished to go and be a regular, normal person. This newly found freedom, she so aspired to achieve, would eventually came with a terrible price, Guilt!

With a tormented heart my mother realized that her escape was only a change of scenery, her imprisonment and torment now existed within her own mind. Where once an overbearing parent stood in strict Judgment of her life, now stands an ideology

12

imbedded within her very soul, ever strict and unyielding as any parent.

How feeble the human being is, becoming a product of its environment, adopting what is taught, with lips of protest unconsciously accepting the plan for its life. With reason and understanding, knowing the truth but painfully accepting the lie.

No sex to a near adolescence young man is similar to denying him his daily bread. An unbearable situation if I may interject from personal experience. Correction, I should say little sex, for a man can be demanding, and my older brother and two older sisters were soon born. What a burden my mother must have felt, with the conception of every child believing she had done something dirty and sinful, placing her very soul in jeopardy of everlasting hell.

Marriage is a Beautiful thing!

Gods plan for the married couple is wholesome and beautiful, he states within his word, deny not your spouse the natural needs of the flesh. If you are married it should be an incredible passionate experience. Fulfilling the needs and lusts of the flesh is essential to the physical health of the married couple. Nurturing the physical and spiritual love for one another, exploring the wonderful feelings and sensations that God has created into the human body, as a married couple is absolutely legal in Gods book. God made the sexual experience for the gratification and enjoyment of his people.

I once read a nearly X-rated book, it was quite graphic and told a story of love and physical passion, a true celebration of the human sexual experience. A graphic portrayal of two lovers drunken with the passions of one another's naked bodies. Take a look at the Song of Solomon before you come to any conclusions.

Grandma and Grandpa were overjoyed with the birth of the grand children, that is after they were born, you see a pregnant woman should be concealed from the world, after all sex is on Gods most hated activities list to the Pentecostal. Out of desperation to escape the confines of a "Godly home" and without careful consideration of the ramifications of choosing just any mate, my family was started, it was 1960.

Wayman was about 5'10" tall, very handsome, from a Pentecostal home and drove a beautiful new convertible. Jewell met Wayman, some six years into her marriage with Robert. While working in a small diner in Carlinville, my mother had the chance to meet Wayman, his handsome looks and warm, friendly personality immediately stole her heart. Suffering from a loveless marriage Jewell was emotionally desperate for life. This young energetic flirtatious boy was beautiful to her soul.

Wayman was a stark opposite to Robert whose normal daily activities included napping, television and smoking, with seldom any deviation. Within a few months they were married, followed a few days later by a divorce from Robert, (affairs of man were so easy before computers).

Making the most of the situation, and suffering from little female affections, Robert promptly took up residences with Wayman's former girlfriend. A true Payton Place drama was unfolding in this wholesome little town of Carlinville, Illinois. The family was starting over, with a man Jewell truly loved and with his religious background maybe he would understand and respect the difficulties within her nature. Maybe she could be normal beside him and enjoy all that life had to offer, at least the love for him within her heart felt very good.

There are no words to describe the feelings one experiences with that first true love. Unbridled Euphoria! Is as close as I can come.

Life with Wayman, while being very emotionally satisfying was quickly becoming difficult for my mother physically. Wayman's seemingly unquenchable desire for sex was stretching her prayers to the limit. Not just sex, new and different forms of sex, well new for her, how could God possible tolerate such behavior, I am surly going to be damned to eternal hell, she thought.

Wayman while being a kind and gentle man, did have his passions and he simply would not tolerate any lack of female satisfaction, if his wife could not perform he would simple go elsewhere.

I heard a funny but seemingly true fable once. It stated that when God created man he programmed him to go to and fro on the earth and sow his seed. But when God programmed woman he programmed her to limit fertilizing to only one farmer. A seemingly odd couple!

Shortly there after Wayman, suffering from a less than a satisfying sex life, began making friendly advances on my mother's cousin. I often wonder "what was he thinking" his wife's own cousin, undeniable lust or just plain ignorance.

Jewell had made a big mistake, evident by her husband's infidelity, obvious inability to understand her lack of ability in the bedroom, and unwillingness to stand beside her and accept her shortcomings. While she loved and adored him, Waymans infidelity and often lack of income were emotionally devastating and above all placing her children in jeopardy.

My mother, with a broken spirit and a broken heart returned to Robert and was soon remarried, all the while caring me inside her. It would be some twenty five years before I learned of my real father Wayman, I am grateful to have met him before he died; the resemblance was remarkable in every fashion.

Father, do the children pay for the sins of the parents? Only in the world of the flesh, my son, be careful what you bring into your life because familiar spirits and demons can find refuge within your family. "I will curse those who hate me to the forth generation, thus sayeth God".

17

Shortly after I was born we moved from Illinois to Charleston South Carolina, Robert was in the Air force and had received orders to go to Vietnam. Our growing family now numbered 5 children, and we had all settled into a small house at 202 Donwood Drive. Our home was the third house on the third row of a brand new subdivision located in Ladson, South Carolina. Robert, shortly after arriving was sent to Vietnam to begin his first tour of duty. While he was never a father in any respect to me I do honor and respect the man for his service to this great country.

Robert would later volunteer for two additional tours in combat, only a piece of lead in the back would eventually bring him home. I later learned from a former service buddy of his, that the needs that were never met at home were quite easily relieved over there. It's no wonder he stayed, speaking from experience one's demons can be quite domineering and demanding. I hold no judgment towards Robert for his time away, war is a difficult time and those who serve are true American heroes. Maybe the third tour was a bit much!

Life at Donwood drive was not easy, money and food were both in short supply, my mother found work at a local sewing factory and Roberts's allotment just covered the mortgage. We were alone! My mother's most unbearable predicament, ranking higher than even sex, being alone. One truly doesn't get intimate with their demons until they are alone, it's at that time their presence is very clear. My mother imparted this unbearable loneliness to me, the worst of my moral failures and less than honorable activities always took place when I was alone. Just as she did I now tremble at the prospect of being alone.

We were alone except for this very nice young man who lived three houses down. His name was Charles, he was short, very handsome and very young, nearly 10 years junior to my mother. Charles was married with two young girls and one very abusive wife. On many occasions he would come to the corner lot and play baseball with us kids. I later learned his wife would lock him out of the house for hours at a time, being the gentle man he was, he suffered the situation. Unremarkable to us kids Charles started playing with us more and more, actually coming to the house hanging around. I have few memories before him and what a wonderful father he would become.

Soon after, my mother once again divorced Robert to pursue a real love, not just a convenient arrangement.

Life with Charles was happy and satisfying, he was young and full of life, my mother loved him and he was as good a man a humanly possible, for we do know "there are no good men, no not one". As I understand things a compromise was established, while sex was still dirty and sinful I guess my mother decided it was a necessary evil to endure a happy marriage. And they did enjoy much happiness, I am forever thankful for Charles Tuckers participation in my life. We were now a real family, we promptly moved back to Illinois and started life anew.

My mother's childhood was overbearing and full of rules and rigid expectations with serious eternal threats of consequence. How she hated the doctrine so, but believing it to be true decided our family would uphold some of the same values. Out of ignorance of truth and warped by the doctrine of man, countless generations have suffered the harsh whip of mistaken and abusive theology.

Chapter Two

My Memories.

From the beginning my most favorite place in this world was church! As a child I was always involved in church, adopting the same rigorous set of rules that my mother had long ago ran away from. My summers were spent with my Grandparents, what a glorious time that was, despite the rigorous indoctrination I would not trade anything for the summers spent in their home.

There are no sweeter memories in my mind, and how I often wish I could be there again. My Grandmother's devotion to God was saintly, when Jesus said "there are no good men" he specifically thought of her and made the statement gender biased. What a beautiful spirit she had and forever I will be grateful for her teachings. While misguided and harsh Ellen Hunt's core doctrine of salvation was rock solid, and not being a learned woman, its origins were unmistakable. It was during one summer with my Grandparents and about the age of eight that I decided I wanted to become a preacher. Little did I know I was departing on a mission that would evolve into an epic lifelong battle for purity and holiness that would spill over into the innocent lives of others.

While slightly mischievous and rambunctious I was basically a very good child. Obviously my parents endured the usual juvenile infractions, and I never received a beating I didn't deserve, and there were many. Possibly the severity of the correction for the misdeeds led to the lack of misconduct. A lesson long forgotten in today's society! That, and the constant voice within my head telling me I was sinning and going to hell. My God was a harsh God, unyielding and complete in his wrath, while I realized this, the alternative was even worse, hell. All I had to do was to be good enough, ask forgiveness for every infraction immediately, lest I die before I do, and I would get to go to Heaven.

For I was taught early, there are no bad people in heaven, there are none that curse, non that smoke, non that drink and non that had sex and died before they asked forgiveness, always be kind and respectful and make sure your at Church every time the doors are open.

This didn't seem too hard as a young boy, and I preached this doctrine to all who would listen. As a child there was nothing within my harsh doctrine that would convince me of anything other than the fact that I was preaching Gods will. As a young boy what I wished myself to do I was basically able to do, or at least get pretty close.

As a teenager life became complicated, while my doctrine was ever there and ever ridged the first of my demons would show its dreadful face. A gift from my father, a man I did not even know, I still operated under the assumption that Robert was my dad. I guess hidden lies to avoid embarrassing family issues had been forgiven long ago. As my father before me did, I soon realized an unquenchable desire for the ladies, a demon that would torment me all the days of my life.

Quite early I had realized the joys of ones own body, almost by accident and purely by experimentation. After the initial realization and explicit pleasure, there was absolutely no possible return to the innocence of a normal 12 year old child. Everyday was another opportunity to experience that wonderful thing that I had learned to do. At my age, and with the rigid regulations and extraordinary list of forbidden fruits that were absolutely taboo and destructive to my very soul, it was no wonder that the slightest hint of impropriety or worldly behavior was a physically exciting experience.

Unfortunately I was blessed with a vivid, colorful imagination, one of astounding clarity and detail, fully capable of doing things that were forbidden to my reality, with respect to the confines of my religion, without physically doing them. To this day I can drive down city streets in my mind and see all of the detail of the houses, trees and all of the aspects of the surrounding amenities from memories of places long ago. With respect to memories my imagination is truly a gift and constant companion but in retrospect the darker less productive abuses of the talent lent to the further determent of my soul and carnal situation.

As I became a teenager I began to realize that I would become aroused simple by thinking about doing one of the many forbidden vices that were so rigidly prohibited within my faith. The physical experience and pleasure that followed would soon become a self feeding ever deepening and destructive "theocoses" (my own word for a destructive psychosis brought about by a well intentioned but flawed theology). The imagination would suffice for a time, but the continued experience would require more creativity and eventual participation.

A messenger to the heathen once wrote, and I paraphrase: to imagine it is the same as doing it! While I trust this mans opinions completely, there is a slight degree of difference. His intention here was to show the folly in even attempting to make the flesh holy.

I was 15 years old and home alone! The usual thoughts and fantasies had left me slightly less aroused than anticipated and the desire to reach new levels of satisfaction was very powerful. Say it! The voice in my head said, just say it, no one will no! Say it, can't you feel the excitement of tasting the forbidden fruit? Say it!

As the first syllables of the very first curse word that had ever uttered out of my mouth came forward, a rush of sexual pleasure so powerful rushed through my body, no sooner than I had said three or four more, my anticipation was fulfilled and the session came to an end.

After what I would come to remember as, the day the man of God died ended, I spent the remainder of the afternoon in my room crying and begging Gods forgiveness. How could I have said those things, oh my God I am so sorry, please forgive me lord, please don't send me to eternal hell. For days the incredible guilt, total disbelief and absolute disappointment was astonishing,

I would never be a good enough man now, I can't believe I have done this forbidden act.

Once not long ago, as a child with puffed up religious arrogance, I actually believed I could go thru life and never utter a single forbidden word. Repeat performances soon became common, all followed by the same remorse and self esteem robbing guilt provided by the first, there was no hope for me except to say my prayers and hope I didn't die before I did.

This simple act of saying words made evil by men would serve my demons well over the next several years. Consider the origin of the words in question, bare with me a moment this may be hard for some of you to even read, but it must be explained to bring about simplicity and understanding of how absolutely absurd and almost comical this legalists venue has become.

Origins of Curse words

(S*H*I*T) Origin 16th Century, Acronym, Meaning "Ship High In Transit" The label "S*H*I*T" was painted on shipping crates containing manure used for fertilizer. If one of these crates were to come in contact with sea water during the voyage, a dangerous explosive gas could be produced. Here we have a simple useful term, only by its very nature associated with animal feces, which was made obscene and forbidden over the years by simple religious fanaticism. Think of the poor sailors who were required to use this acronym on a daily basis; ever heard the term curses like a sailor?

(F*U*C*K) Origin Middle Ages England, Acronym, Meaning "Fornication Under Consent of the King" For a time in feudal England the Kings control over the lives of his subjects was absolute and complete. This control for years even reached into the peasants bedrooms. A man wishing to have sexual relations with his wife was required to gain a permit from the local governor. Worse than that, one was required to hang this permit on the front door of his dwelling during the affair. I'm quite certain the sign (F*U*C*K) hanging on ones door raised an eyebrow or two in the village and probably a slap on the back at the local pub afterwards.

Regardless, the point I am trying to make is these words among others of even less interesting origins were and are part of everyday life and language. These have no origins of any evil or satanic overtone; they were not created in hell to add to the filth of the human condition nor were they conceived to be stumbling blocks to "Godly Men".

Purely said, religion made them evil, religion made them illegal to Gods people, just as religion has done for so many wonderful and enjoyable past times such as dancing, wine, sex and music. To what end, shackle another soul to a belief, create another forbidden fruit to add to mans temptation, as if there doesn't exist enough already, for no other reason than a vain attempt to control and to make the flesh holy.

Considering the present day religious and moral societal taboos in place, I would never condone such words to be used in public nor do I use them myself. My examples here are for an understanding of how simple, innocent "things", for a lack of a better word, can be twisted and made evil by the doctrines of well meaning, ignorant purveyors of religious doctrine.

I would learn years later that the entire English language is repulsive to God, in comparison to his heavenly language; no one word is any more despicable than any other. Why then did men choose to single certain words out and create such a controversy? The only reference to this in Gods word is a passage telling Christians not to be crude.

I once heard of a man, born of a virgin they said, he came to tear down rules and laws that acted as

*binding shackles on his people, I guess since he left
they have had time to build some more.*

In 1983 at the age of 16 my family moved again to South
Carolina, seeking employment from a loss of the steel industry
jobs in the mid west. I missed Illinois, it was a wonderful place,
the small towns I grew up in were quaint and wholesome, I did
detest the cold weather and for that reason did not wish to return.

After about six months in the Carolina's my parents were
recalled to work in Illinois and decided to return north once again.
South Carolina was good for me, the warm weather was
wonderful and the academic requirements to graduate high school
were far below those of Illinois. In fact as a junior I needed only
two additional credits to graduate, plus I had a girl friend. After a
heated battle with my mother I waived goodbye as they drove
away, leaving me alone at age sixteen in a very big world.
Freedom had come!

After my parents left South Carolina I was living at Roberts's
house in Summerville. One of the absolute worst days of my life
was about to come into play. It was the middle of the night and I
was alone, aroused as usual I suddenly found myself staring at a
pack of cigarettes someone had left on the table. If there is one

day in my life that I could live over it would be this one, I have suffered more torment and disgust over the results of that night than any other in my life.

I pulled the cigarette out and put it to my lips, my heart was pounding like a freight train I had never been as sexually excited as I was at that moment. The fantasy of doing something has no comparison to the actual act, even with a vivid imagination. In the back of my mind I always new the actual act would never happen, only a fantasy, a tool, I would never allow it, my God would never allow it.

As I smoked my first cigarette the absolute sexual excitement and emotional fascination was incredible, my body actually began to shake uncontrollable almost as if I was freezing, and I did feel cold, extremely cold. The most forbidden act I could possible do and I was doing it, oh God I was doing it, I can't believe it, it feels so good! To my amazement the convulsive nature of my deeds would become a normal part of my acting out. Astonishingly it would never die away or become less pronounced with time or as my acts became more common place.

I often wonder if more than a mental state if the extreme cold and convulsions were due to an uneasy closeness or proximity to a demon. The pleasure most normal people feel from smoking IE:

taste, dizziness, relaxation, were all eclipsed by the emotional frenzy of tasting the forbidden fruit.

The demons within had a party that night, they had satisfied their agenda and successfully shackled the man of God to a foolish fetish that would last nearly a life time. The act in actuality amounted to very little, but in my mind, the legalistic Pentecostal mind, it made me a law breaker, less than a man, especially less than a man of God.

When one smokes a cigarette he or she runs the risk of a physical addiction to the substance, the side affects are detrimental and dangerous to the body, but smoking can never sentence your soul to hell. There is one unpardonable sin and it can not be committed by the body, listen close because this I wager you have never heard before. The unpardonable sin is committed by a person's spirit! When your soul is sent to earth and joined to a human body there is one ultimate purpose for the entire process, a choice! Your spirit must make a choice! Every since the war in heaven and the heavenly hosts chose God or Satan, all of creation has been apart of the ultimate choice. For the express purpose of pledging a true allegiance, your spirit is placed in a body, born unto sin, the nature of all flesh is evil, and your spirit must overcome the flesh and choose good over evil,

God over Satan. In making this choice the flesh is brought into submission by the spirit and the spirit man within you accepts Jesus Christ as the lord of all Creation.

Those who do not accept Christ are the spirits that were never able to over come the nature and carnal pleasures of the flesh long enough to make the only logical choice. Each spirit has until the last dying breath of life is expelled out of the body in which to acknowledge the one true God, after this time the spirit has committed the one unpardonable sin, blasphemy against the Holy Spirit of God, or pronouncing by sustained silence that Satan is their God.

I have heard so many different explanations of the unpardonable sin or as the Bible calls it "Blasphemy against the Holy Spirit". Everything from taking Gods name in vain, to making jokes about the Holy Spirit. The simplicity of its explanation to me seems inescapable. Dying without acknowledging Christ is the same as pronouncing Satan as Lord of all, thus your spirit has committed Blasphemy against Gods Holy Spirit. In supporting doctrine God says "all flesh is an abomination to me" how can something so abominable possibly rise to the level of actually possessing the ability to even speak or commune with God?

With absolute assurance I tell you the only part of you that God has any interest in is your spirit, the ranting of the flesh he will never entertain nor acknowledge. While the flesh is capable of untold atrocities and absolute abomination, it is the guiding light of the spirit inside that is supposed to temper the nature of the beast and bring about a controlling acknowledgement of the truth of creation. Thus I say to you, among the many despicable acts the flesh is capable of, none will rise to the level of hell or the unforgivable sin, that abomination must be committed by you, the spirit man inside.

I was once told about a man, a criminal I think he was, who at the last few moments of his life looked into Jesus' eyes and proclaimed him Lord of all. That man is in heaven now, Jesus said so. The other criminal that was present did not make the same decision, he is in hell now, the unpardonable sin he committed, by allowing his flesh to die without ever acknowledging the deity of the living God, the very one that had made him. A choice that must be made!

Chapter three

The compromise

Frances was average, warm and friendly and I adored her. I adored her to the detriment of my morale convictions, convictions I had long sense cemented within my soul. After all as a child they had seemed so easy, a boy does what a boy wishes, if I wish to do good I do good, why should it be any different for a young man. It was different, I was consumed with lust, all I thought about was kissing her more, exploring ever deeper into the realm of sexuality, and asking forgiveness on an hourly basis lest I die and go to hell before I did. The torment had begun, a demon so powerful, so capable and so ancient, and to my amazement and disgust I was entertaining him.

As it has always been, boys and girls left alone eventually cross all lines, as we soon did. I have never experienced such excitement and passion, followed shortly there after by tremendous torment and guilt. A conflict of emotion, my first love made no allowance for any other, and he would send me to hell for not following his rigid and explicit rules. Out of torment and over time, the first of many compromises of appeasement to demons were established. Frances, convicted slightly by her faith understood the tears I would shed, but the mutual physical attraction was overpowering, a compromise would have to be made.

We together decided that sex after marriage was ok, we couldn't get married, so we made vows to each other. Believing this act of unofficial marriage would relieve my overshadowing guilt and conviction, we proceeded down a slippery road and threw caution to the wind, it would prove to be a futile effort.

I once read about a man that had a woman's husband killed, so that he could conceal the adulteress affair with the woman, I'm sure he is in heaven because God himself said, he was a man after his own heart, surly my sins don't raise to such a level. Or do they?

The aspirations and goals of an aspiring preacher are such, at least in my mind, that I must be better than the rest, I must be holy and righteous, how else could I possible preach the gospel one day. I was determined to marry this woman, make amends to God and get on with becoming a minister. This "demon of lust for women" would have to be defeated, by marriage, because God hadn't taken him away as requested, I would do it myself.

Over all I would say that as a teenager I was again a good kid! I never attended a single party, never drank alcohol, absolutely no bad language, at least none that anyone had ever heard, and would do nothing less than honorable in public.

Have you ever done something that you knew was wrong or illegal? And getting away with the crime was tremendously exciting almost arousing?

Well everything was illegal for me, religiously, with far greater consequences than that imposed by men in the correction of human laws. I was realizing that the things that I hate would excite me, a rush of adrenaline to the level of sexual passion would envelope my flesh at the thought of simple saying a bad word or doing something forbidden by my religion. During times alone the thoughts soon turned to actions and deeds, in support of my ever increasing need for sexual excitement, but never in public, what a hypocrite I had become.

Just as the forbidden fruit was a temptation beyond the abilities of Adam and Eve, anything that is forbidden to the human flesh becomes a temptation, the more forbidden the greater the flesh wishes to consume. To a Pentecostal there is nothing more forbidden than the vices of the flesh!

I was seventeen years old out of school and making $3.25 dollars per hour working for the city of Summerville, I was going to ask Frances to marry me. After careful consideration, this was the logical strategy, I would kill two demons with one attack, my morals would again be intact, I would never be alone again and I could enjoy sex without guilt as often as I liked.

My proposal plans involved the age old process of asking the parent's for permission, a less than enjoyable endeavor.

No, absolutely no, Frances is going to college, I forbid her to marry you, in fact if she does she can forget about our support. Her mother's words I will never forget, sitting in her kitchen and receiving such rejection was heart breaking. At least Frances was

not here, I reasoned, I can ask her myself, regardless of her
mother's opinion.

I never seen Frances again, a note was placed in my mail box
late that night along with my class ring, a difficult time. The
events of that autumn ended my marriage prospects, it ended my
relationship as well. It would be 18 years before I would see
Frances again. As we sat in a café' she told me the tragic events
of her life, domestic difficulties, her husbands incarceration, and
how she had always regretted the decision to leave me.

My heart was broken as I too deeply regretted that decision,
but as too many children often realize, parents don't always know
what is best. In fact most parents have difficulty managing their
own lives let alone their grown children's. With hindsight and
understanding I now know I never had any chance to be with
Frances. Her mother came from Old Summerville blue blood
money and her father was a Naval Captain, I was simply a poor
boy destined for commonality and poverty, at least in their eyes. I
would later hear that her father ran off with his secretary and her
mother was waiting tables at a roadside café. I take no enjoyment
in the hardships her parents have endured, I only marvel in the
fact that their own home and marriage was in disarray and only an
illusion of happiness. Considering their position and mistakes

they still chose to make life long decisions about their daughter's happiness.

I remember Jesus referring someone to an optometrists concerning a similar situation.

Now alone and with a broken heart, at this time my prospects for life somewhat shaken and my passions lonesome for the lost affections I had grown so accustomed too. It's quite easy to survive the loneliness physically, emotionally and morally it's a devastating storm with life long prospects.

I was soon attempting to satisfy my desires in any way possible, the longer you entertain an act the more familiar and comfortable it becomes. At a certain point it may actually consume and define you, no longer being something that you do, instead now something that you are. With this in mind I began to realize the demons associated with the faith of my fathers were substantial and quite capable. A secular scholar would call them fetishes, a demon by any other name is still an evil minion.

I once read about a man, the greatest of twelve, he also done things that he hated when he was alone. To his credit he choose a companion to accompany him on his travels, I think God blesses the desire to do good, regardless of the outcome.

Gods Perfect Gift of Marriage

God's perfect plan for marriage is an incredible and perfect design when followed. You see Gods intention for man and woman is that they should abstain from physical and sexual contact until they are married. In doing so neither would experience anything more gratifying than that of their spouse. The physical love between the two would be the greatest either had ever enjoyed, providing complete and unconditional physical contentment. Unfortunately one only receives a single attempt at doing it right, mine was gone, though Frances and I were not married we were the only ones both had ever been with, and the physical relationship was incredible. Had we married I truly believe I would have received Gods perfect gift of Marriage.

Frances was gone and I was alone, dipping deeper and deeper into the personal soul destroying moral deficiencies of my less than honorable activities. My ideals were high, my convictions deep, my goals long ago established, but my ability to manage my alone time was non existent. God would surly make a special trip to earth very soon to personally cast me into hell, or grind me into saw dust, depending on his mood that day. I often think of Frances, but to my discredit I seldom remember any activities outside of the bedroom, thank you father for your un-intentional gift of lust that you passed on to me, with sarcasm I say it has been a source of great excitement and torment.

Regardless of ones values they are the guiding azimuth in ones personal life, good bad or indifferent, each set of values will set ones feet on a path. As each of my rigidly established religious values began to erode, my opinion of myself also began to erode, how can the great man of God who can never remember a time when Jesus was not a part of his life, fail? Not just fail, fail time and time again, day after day the same broken record playing out time and time again.   Unfortunately compromise is sometimes easier than correction, especially when one is alone and full of teenage hormones.

Chapter Four

In the Army.

As a boy I had always had a great fascination and admiration for soldiers. My patriotic fervor for this grand and glorious country would be a life long obsession also, thankfully a well received one. My friends and I would spend countless hours running around the woods shooting our toy guns at one another, our biggest concern at the time was who got to be the American soldier. As an answer to a broken heart and a secondary dream I soon found myself in the United States Army.

Life in training at Ft McClellan Alabama in August of 1985 was difficult, not to mention HOTT! but overall the experience was quite enjoyable, at a minimum I was seldom alone. Barracks life was good and afforded me little private time in which to indulge my demons. The Army soon assigned me to the National Security Agency at fort Meade Maryland, it was a very easy duty assignment, I found a very good Pentecostal church and attempted to resume my life and goals.

I was a soldier now, very proud and capable, Army life was quite easy for me. Duty and barracks life filled my days with companions, but the demons were always present, waiting in the shadows for the opportunity to speak softly into my mind. Flesh, biding its time to dominate the spirit, the age old battle that all men face and very few acknowledge.

I have heard of a man, the greatest of all, who prepared for battle with Satan himself, the preparation took 40 days. Forty days to place the flesh into total submission to the spirit, how could one possible maintain this type of spiritual combat readiness?

Gods Glorious Green Mountain.

In the Christian walk there are various levels, I compare this to a mountain and a climber, most Christians climb about a quarter of the way up and make camp. Their campsite is slightly above heathen activities and considerably below the heights of wisdom, understanding, strength and power. As you ascend to higher and higher levels your closeness to the Holy Spirit and your understanding of Gods plan and purpose for your life become clearer with each step. Reaching the summit you will receive absolute peace, understanding, spiritual gifts and a closeness with your heavenly father beyond any feeling you have experienced with you earthly body.

At various times I have achieved incredible heights within my daily walk, actually feeling the very power of God within my soul. Unfortunately just as the patriarchs of the Bible also experienced, this height of spiritual awareness and authority does not seem to be sustainable for long periods of time.

If any man tells you he has achieved the heights of the mountain of Gods power and remains in his presence, I would wager him to be a liar, a one in a million saint or simply ignorant

44

of understanding. While the view from the summit of Gods Glorious green mountain is like nothing you have ever experienced, with every decent it seems to become harder and harder to make the climb again.

One summer while camping near the bottom of God's glorious green mountain I took leave from the Army and returned home to Charleston. My age old battles were raging and the loneliness and desires were destroying my soul.

While in town I went to visit my mother at the clothing store she was managing at the time, while there I was introduced to a young lady who was in her employment.

Renee' was average, a single mom with a two year old daughter, after our introduction we decided to go out to dinner before I left town. During our dinner date I realized Renee' and Nikki her daughter, were living at a woman's shelter, the news broke my heart. She seemed to be a nice girl, obviously very different ideals and beliefs from mine, but very nice and her daughter was adorable. Over the next couple of days the thoughts of the two of them living in a shelter was devastating to me, was I supposed to help them? The Army didn't pay much, I was just surviving myself. Could I help them and myself at the same time? After all, I had a good heart, she needed salvation and I think I

could love anyone! And I could have sex with out being
convicted and sentenced to hell.

Out of pity for her, pity for myself, and desperate to revive my
moral ambitions, I asked Renee' to marry me. Out of sheer
economic desperation she said yes! Two weeks later we walked
into a courtroom in Annapolis Maryland, as I held Nikki in my
arms, I entered into the most holy of unions with little regard for
choice of mate and the consequences there of. Regally attempting
save a desperate mother and child from cold and hunger I easily
justified the decision. The personal desire to escape the confines
of my self convicted deviant behavior was also a driving
justification, expecting to finally relieve my sexual desire within
the laws of my intolerant and harsh God, I said my vows.

The first couple of weeks of married life were ok, we settled
into an apartment and began playing house. Two strangers only
thirty days before apparently joined in life's little adventures for
the duration. Unfortunately the curse of pre-marital sex
immediately reared its ugly head, she was nothing compared to
Frances, sex with Renee' was almost a nasty experience. I
suddenly realized sex was more than just an act to be preformed
with strangers. It matters in a tremendous way with whom you are

intimate, if there are no loving affections it can be a vile and dirty experience.

Renee' wasted little time settling into her old routines or at least wanting to. Let's go out drinking, she asked one night! While this was a vice I had been completely successful in confining there was no way I would ever do this in public, nor would my wife. The clash of cultures soon became intolerable and the marriage was dissolved within 10 weeks.

I remember my first experience with alcohol, the arousal of the forbidden fruit was very strong and stimulating. But thankfully the available fruit was a very harsh whiskey, and the taste almost dissolved my tongue. That ended that!

Renee' did now have an apartment and a job, a used car and a new start in life, I took some comfort in the fact her and Nikki were better off. One part of the plan was moderately successful I had indeed rescued this mother and child. One month after the divorce Renee contacted me and asked for money to get an abortion. With little regard I financed an abomination to my moral stature. Regret of regrets, how quickly the young make such foolish decisions. I was alone again and the enormous

baggage I now carried ever eroded my ability to achieve the
heights of religious fortitude that I aspired too and I thought were
once possible.

*"Suffer the little children unto me" thank you Lord
for caring for the little ones so carelessly discarded.
May I ever suffer under the rod for the despicable and
deliberate act that was purchased by me!*

My life long dream of preaching the gospel was now so very
far away, after all, divorce is the one unforgivable sin within the
Christian hypocrisy, excuse me, Church. It has never failed to
amaze me, Christians will drive hundreds of miles to see a former
axe murdering rapist, who found salvation out of terror while
being passed around a prison bunk room, preach. Then turn up
there judgmental snotty noses at a man who wishes to preach the
gospel after having a divorce.

After all, it's in the Bible "a bishop shall be a man of one
wife" nothing in there about a bishop shall not be a former axe
murderer. The hypocrisy of the church in this respect stems from
a desire to see their leaders pure and faultless, not from an
accurate rendering of scripture. A careful reading of the passage
will conclude that the meaning was "only one wife at a time", for

a bishop has no time for his flock if he has 3 or 4 wives. I will wager that any man of one wife can attest to this truth and wholeheartedly agree.

"It's in the Bible" this cliché is despicable to me, 99% of Christians don't know what's "in the Bible", they don't study and prefer to let men tell them "what's in the Bible". Seek and you shall find, trust no man in your search for truth.

I once heard of a man, the son of God they said, he came to forgive all sins with no exclusions, how soon his so called followers have forgotten.

After my latest debacle I once again threw myself into my religion, determined to reach new heights and conquer old enemies. My church was exciting and warm and I spent every possible moment there. This was a good season, my strength was high and my demons at bay. Still in the Army and ready for a vacation it was time for a trip back to Charleston.

49

While back home on leave I ran into a girl I had dated one time in high school, my meeting Frances had curtailed any further dating activity with this girl. Rebecca was a cute girl about average and very Baptist. My intentions were innocent and we began a long distance friendship. Letters and phone calls occupied the next couple of months along with a few road trips home. Becky was a nice girl living with her parents in an apartment in Summerville, a nice girl sporting a very heavy burden. Some unspeakable things had been and were being done to her in her father's house, and she cried out for help.

We had barely corresponded for three months when it was decided we should get married. She needed to get out of her fathers house, immediately. Also, she was a religious girl, she needed immediate help, and I had a good heart and could love anyone, who was of a similar religious culture, the later being added to my mindset. And as before the lustful demon of sex could be tamed with a willing partner, married partner that is. We were married in her Baptist church and that day departed for Maryland. Once again I had entered into the most holy of unions with little regard for the ramifications of not choosing a mate cautiously or with any consideration for love, a rescue mission once again.

Life with Becky was somewhat tolerable, the sex was ok, at least it was not nasty. Our lives were very busy, or at least mine was. Working the night shift at the base and running a small construction company during the day. Becky worked part time at the local Burger King and attended community college in the evenings. Time at home seemed to be non existent or for a specific purpose. Slowly over the course of the next few months she began to become quite withdrawn and depressed.

Taken from her environment, regardless of its problems, she did have friends and her mother and sister. All of that was gone now, she was basically alone. I would occasionally find her sitting in a room staring at the wall, demanding to move back to South Carolina, and becoming frigid and cold. Had we tendered a real relationship there may have been emotional ties that could have helped the situation and possibly remedied the problems. To inflate the situation I was in the Army and could not move back home for another year. With the absence of love and the reality of two strangers living together there was little hope for any future relationship.

Within the course of 15 months I had married and divorced twice, added to the moral and emotional baggage I carried; and basically allowed myself to slip further down the slopes of Gods

Glorious Green Mountain that I so desperately wanted to climb. From then on I vowed my days of rescuing females in trouble were over, I would find a wife the right way, fall in love first.

Chapter five

The Adult years.

After my enlistment was over I soon returned to Charleston and started a small construction company building houses. Hurricane Hugo had just destroyed the low country and business was extremely good. I had no church home and my walk with God was virtually non existent. After all, I was a really bad man now, I sported two divorces, among other despicable acts, two monumental anchors lashed around my neck, after all there is no greater sin in the Christian church than divorce, or so they think.

That summer I was spending a fair amount of time at Robert's house, still thinking he was my father, he had remarried and his wife's daughter was living with them. Sherry was a knock out, beautiful, fashionable and quite glamorous, and eleven years my senior. We quietly tendered a relationship without the knowledge of the family and I genuinely fell in love with this woman.

Sherry had more than her share of problems, suffering from Manic Depression and constantly taking controlling medications, but the excitement she instilled within me was more than a trade. One night about 1am her oldest son of 13 came down the stairs to find his mother sitting on his step uncle's lap, facing the wrong direction. Needless to say it was an interesting night, the secret was out and I really didn't care.

After about a year we were married and I moved my new family, wife and three kids, into a small country home. Aside from the bouts of depression and the occasional violent outbursts associated, life was nice. Sherry was a good lover, there was never a time that she did not try to satisfy my extraordinary desires. She was an incredible mix, going to church with me on Sunday and talking dirty too me in bed, there was little in my closet of forbidden vices that she wouldn't perform for me. And still the conflict raged, only different now, horrible conviction for the deviant behavior, at least deviant in my mind. I was married now, to a woman whom I loved, whom I enjoyed having sex with, but still the man of God cannot do these things. It's ok to have sex with your wife but keep it very civilized, almost missionary; my indoctrinated mind would tell me. My demons exploited each and every legal loophole they could find, I would fix one problem and they would convict me of another. It seemed I could not win!

We did have a reasonable life together laughing and loving, fighting and surviving, all the while attempting to strive for at least a minimal level of religious satisfaction. After several years of marriage sherry's two boys had become teenager's very disobedient teenagers. Stealing the car or coming home drunk were everyday occurrences and to my amazement she had little regard for there activities, or trying to curtail them. My house was a mess, I had two amoral teenage boys running the place, their mother covering for them and empowering them in most cases, or just not caring at all. Life had suddenly taken a dramatic and difficult turn, and the prospects for the future did look bleak.

About this time in our relationship I took a job as a traveling technician, installing security systems for the Navy. My new position would thankfully take me away from my troubled home for the next two years.

As we entered our fifth year of marriage my home was in chaos and shattered. Sherry was having increasing difficulty dealing with her illness and the troubles of the children. Her emotional problems evident by her being placed in a mental institution in the recent year, and the children running wild in and out of our home.

I was working on the road, I completely hated coming home, and the passion that once existed between Sherry and I was replaced by resentment and disgust. Spare the rod and spoil the child, I don't think Sherry ever owned a rod.

Faced with the obvious, divorce; we decided to attempt marriage counseling to fix our problems. I will never forget this time and the counseling sessions in which we attended, three to be exact. I had found a Christian psychologist, believing only a religious person could possibly help us, and hoping for some good results we began our therapy.

Loud and dangerous, good adjectives among others, to describe the first two counseling sessions we participated in. After the final day and my wife's numerous violent outbreaks, scaring the councilor at times I believe. The Doctor pulled me aside and said "I'm done, and you would have to be a sociopath to live with that woman". I wasn't shocked I guess I had gotten used to the violence she displayed; the exciting side of her had tempered the effects. Unfortunately the exciting side was gone now, never to return.

Shortly there after I was preparing for a 12 month trip to California. My job would be to install a security system at the Navy base at China Lake, California. Before my departure and in our sixth year of marriage it was decided we should divorce. With a feeling of relief from the fighting and the constant confusion I left for California and did not look back.

During my marriage to Sherry the heavy burden which my mother carried, concerning my fathers true identity, had become too much for her, with tearful eyes she divulged the truth about my real father. With incredible disbelief I immediately realized the truth, something I had wondered about for years.

I was nothing like my siblings, they were ordinary, average in a good respect, slightly docile and never straying from home. With exception of Sarah the wild one, there's a rebel in every family, her early rebellious behavior was as extreme as my early religious behavior. My siblings didn't posses the passion and drive that I seemed to aspire too, and on the other side they didn't posses the extraordinary lust and desire either. Or at least they were very good about concealing it.

Sarah how seemingly wise you appear to me now, your wild years have tempered into a beautiful mix of Godliness and wisdom. While my Godly years have evolved into seemingly less than honorable behavior, and a resume' of failure. I wish I had maybe sown a few wild oats as a teenager as you did, and maybe my latter years would be more sublime. I take great pride in having at least some part in your understanding of the true nature of God and salvation. My beautiful sister whom I love unconditionally you remind me more everyday of our beloved Grandmother!

Chapter Six

My Father.

Wayman Meredith stood in his driveway, no shirt and working on a lawn mower the day I arrived. Unannounced was my arrival, It was my desire to see what this man was really like, giving him notice would only allow for a less than accurate conclusion. Human nature tends to place its best foot forward for the strangers of the world to see. My plan was simple, walk up, shake his hand and introduce myself. Wayman had only seen me as a child once, in a crowded auction house from a distance in Carlinville. Strangely I remember the man smiling and waving at me, I wondered at the time if I was who he was waving at.

My uncle Don, my mother's brother who lived in the same area, had agreed to accompany me to Waymans house. While my idea for an unannounced meeting with my birth father was bold, I still didn't posses the guts to go alone. Uncle Don and I strolled up the driveway of a very rural farm house and as I approached, Wayman turned and looked me in the face.

The plan, the scenario I had played over in my mind so many times in the last few weeks, wasn't working very well, I could say nothing, no introduction just a blank stare came from my face. I found myself looking at my own face 20 years older, what a powerful realization. As the tears began to swell in my eyes he put his arms around me and said "I know you son".

I will never forget my feelings over the entire occasion, meeting a total stranger and feeling an immediate connection if not kinship, more than just a revelation and meeting of ones father, a spiritual recognition of a long lost friend. Over the course of the afternoon and to my amazement I would realize how similar both our lives had been. Early on, Wayman's Pentecostal convictions were many, and over a lifetime they were slowly eroded away by an unquenchable lust and the in ability to be a good enough person, followed by the associated self conviction and personal destruction of the moral consequences there of.

Wayman was presently married to wife number five, he told me she was the one and there would be no more, had he not died shortly there after I often wonder what would have become of

Wayman. Either within himself or within one of our forefathers a compromise was made so many years ago. An invitation for a demon to attach itself to a family and bridge the generational gaps, leaping from father to son. Carrying with it the legal regulations of a misguided religion, a tool to snare and shackle the good will and innocent nature of the young and insure their failure in Gods plan for humanity.

There are many demons in the world of men, most people do not realize that spiritual warfare rages in the shadows around all of us. Most don't realize that the more you walk towards the light, the higher you climb on Gods Glorious Green Mountain, the more demons are assigned to bring you down. Demons are very specific in their craft, specializing in different aspects of human nature, just as a person would specialize in a trade or profession. One may specialize in adultery, one in alcoholism, pornography, or homosexuality, I'm sure some even multitask and specialize in several human vices at once. While the demons specialty craft may differ from minion to minion the demons motive and ultimate objective has never changed. This motivation being to claim the souls who have not chosen to follow their creator and to shackle the ones who have. Souls who have not chosen Christ are the remaining treasure to be won within this timeless battle, but shackling the chosen ones is a brilliant move to assure that particular chess piece is out of play and will not influence any of the other pieces.

Many would laugh at the thought of being a pawn in the ultimate universal chess game. With absolute certainly I can assure you that this is the reality of the situation called humanity. Fortunately wither you stay a pawn or become a very powerful piece is entirely in your hands. Unfortunately the sides are not predetermined and you may join which ever side that you choose to serve.

Chess is one of the only games where the number of pieces one has doesn't necessarily dictate the winning side. How and when you decide to use your pieces is the key to victory.

While true Christians can not be entered by demons they are constantly being influenced and tormented. It is a tragic affair when a demon is adopted into a family, and it takes a near miracle to remove it. Wayman eventually accepted his demon, later becoming a hard core biker and hosting legendary hell's angel's parties at his house in the country, from what I have heard they say you could always find a naked woman or two at Waymans house.

So many questions had now been answered, who I am, why I'm like I am, and one possible conclusion to my life, should I follow Wayman's example.

Thank you father for the life that you gave me, I don't blame you for any aspects of my life, I see you fought and lost the same battle that I now fight. May the God of heaven remember you as you were, and not as you ended, rest now.

Chapter Seven

A most excellent season.

After returning home from California my traveling employment had come to an end, the nature of security work often involves layoff and job interruptions. During this time I opened a used car lot in Summerville, buying and selling very used automobiles. Sherry and I had divorced and I was once again alone and as far from my religion as ever. Prospects for the future were uncertain and at this juncture I was hoping to just make a living and get to tomorrow. On my many trips to town I would often stop at the local Checkers restaurant for lunch, there I would find the next chapter of my life.

Marlene was about average, thin with plain features; we began to talk and were soon dating. Marlene had two boys age 8 and 9 from a previous marriage and lived with her children in a small house near the airport.

After a short time dating our relationship became quite friendly, Marlene asked me to move in with her. Though it was against my nature and contrary to my moral beliefs, those things really didn't seem to carry too much weight at the time, I moved in and we began playing house. Marlene was a decent lover, passive and agreeable, allowing me my pleasures with little complaint or refusal. My only reluctance was her monthly visitor which seemed to transform this quite and gentle person into an angry and bitter she devil. Fortunately it lasted only a week and the three remaining weeks were quite amiable.

After about 4 months Marlene became pregnant, a concern we had not even addressed as she had to seek professional assistance conceiving in the past. We immediately made plans to be married before the baby was born. God forbid I bring a child into this world to a single mother.

Alexandria Mercedes, my daughter, the most precious gift God has ever given to a person. As a young man I had never wanted to have children, it was my belief that to have children was a sentence to being poor, and I was going to be comfortable if not wealthy.

My parents had struggled to support and clothe five children and I was determined not to make the same mistake. The day

Alexandria was born my entire outlook on life changed, I was not poor, in fact I felt rich, the richest man in the world. And the women who gave her to me and allowed me to name her, I would grow to love.

Shortly after Alexandria's birth I began to work in the security industry once more, accepting a four month job in Hawaii. Little did I know that would be one of the greatest and most beneficial four months of my life. I was married, back on track with God and had been recently ordained by a small local congregation. A non-denominational church who had the ability to look over ones past sins and focus on ones heart, what a novel if not scriptural idea! It seemed maybe I could reach that next level on God's beautiful glorious green mountain at long last.

Chapter Eight

The Awakening

For some time now I had established a tract ministry as a prelude to starting a church. I would provide religious materials for bus stations, grocery stores and hand outs on street corners. My plans were to continue this ministry while in Hawaii, and I would begin immediately after arriving.

In front of the tourists Market in Waikiki is the most wonderful boulevard, at any moment there are hundreds of people of every nationality imaginable strolling by. It was in front of the market that I first met John Stewart. John was from Sweden and had been a Doctor at one time, as I understand things he ran away from the rat race and adopted a less stressful way of life, and from his general attitude a much more rewarding one also.

After hitchhiking across the United States visiting churches and ministering to people, John found himself in Hawaii. One evening as I walked down the side walk in front of the Market I heard the words of the apostle Paul, spoken in the King James language, and with an elegant Swedish accent.

I will never forget the meeting, John had just read a verse aloud and I immediately answered with the following verse, the exchange went on for two or three courses until I could no longer remember the passage. Our friendship was Immediate, John was a street preacher living on the slopes of the volcano and existing on the charity of tourists. Each day for several hours he would stand in front of the market and read the beautiful words of the Kings James bible, softly and non confrontationally. Occasionally interested persons would ask questions or hand him dollars, he was fed and clothed and considered anything more a blessing.

John was a walking bible encyclopedia, any question asked would immediately be answered, not through personal memory but with scripture. Within moments of the question the bible was open and a passage of relevance was displayed, this was astounding to me. We spoke at length discussing our lives and ambitions, faults and failures. The following night I was invited to share the street corner and begin ministering to the lost.

Taking my place on the crowded street, and with shaking hands I opened my Bible and began to speak, I still to this day do not understand the fear that was within me on that street corner. Absolute terror, a demon of fright and fear attempting to shackle and dismiss the worker of God, thankfully reassurance from John and time would overcome this crafty devil. After several nights the preaching was comfortable and very exciting, at the end of each work day my feet could not get me back to the Market place fast enough.

John's theory on street preaching was simple and genius, he had arranged hundreds of passages which dealt with Gods love and salvation into what read as short stories or beautiful poems. His idea was that you have from 10 to 20 seconds with each of the people that pass by, the most important thing that they could possible hear is Gods very own word. How true this statement was, as I would read the words I would see faces turn and look, some stopping briefly but most just continuing to their destinations.

On one particular night I made an incredible observation, there are several words for God in the Bible, Jehovah, Lord, God, Father, King, and Jesus among others. At the mention of the name Jesus heads would turn, none of the other names had this affect.

The profound nature of this discovery was that of the many different nationalities present, the name Jesus they would all seem to understand. Immediately I began substituting all of the names of God with the Name of Jesus while preaching, and the increase in participation was profound.

Revelation charges "whoa to any man who alters the words of this book" but it also says God the father turned his authority over to Jesus, so I'm hoping he didn't mind my revision.

I preached on the streets of Waikiki nearly every night for about four months, the most satisfying season of my life. In addition to the active preaching John's bible studies had enlightened me to the necessity of daily bible reading. Not just reading, coordinated reading, devouring, over the next three years I would read the Bible through dozens of times. Additionally I was shown the folly of new age bible translations and to this day believe the King James Bible holds power within its words. Some translations, seemingly innocent, change ever so simply the texts meaning, and other text with blatant disregard for the original manuscript attempt to remove the deity of God.

God is a loving Father and wishes to see his people draw near to him, He has provided one perfect translation for every language in the world, anything less would be shameful and unfair, for the English language this is the King James Version.

Study Schedule

Column 1
Genisus 1-4
Matthew 1-4
Job 1-2

Psalms 1-4
Mark 1-4

Proverbs 1
Isaiah 1-4

Luke 1-4
Ec. 1-4

John 1-4
Exodus 1-5
Acts 1-4

Job 3-4
Psalms 5-9
Romans 1-4
Proverbs 2
Isaiah 5-9
1 Cor. 1-4
Solomen 1-4
II Cor. 1-4
Leviticus 1-4
Galatians 1-6

Job 5-6
Psalms 10-14
Ephesians 1-6

Proverbs 3
Isaiah 10-14
Philippians 1-4
II Samuel 1-6
Colossians 1-4
Leviticus 5-14
I Thess. 1-5
Job 7-8
Psalms 15-19
II Thes. 1-3
Proverbs 4
Isaiah 15-19
I Timothy 1-6
Lamentations 1-5

II Timothy 1-4
Deuteronomy 1-4

Titus 1-3
Job 9-10
Psalms 20-24

Exodus 6-14

I Samuel 1-6
**Philimon
+Heb.1-4**

Column 2
Proverbs 5
Isaiah 20-24
James 1-5

Ezekial 1-6
I Peter 1-5

Joshua 1-5
II Peter 1-3

Job 11-12
Psalms 25-29

I John 1-5
Proverbs 6
Isaiah 25-29
**II +III John +
Jude**
Daniel 1-4
Genisus 5-10
Revelation 1-4
Judges 1-5
Matthew 5-9
Job 13-14
Psalms 30-34
Mark 5-9
Proverbs 7

Isaiah 30-34
Luke 5-9
Hosea 1-4

John 5-9
Ruth 1-4
Acts 5-9
Ezekial 7-14
Job 15-16
Psalms 35-39
Romans 5-9
Proverbs 8
Isaiah 35-39
I Cor. 5-9
Joel 1-3
II Cor. 5-9
I Samuel 7-14

Galatians 1-6
Job 17-18

Psalms 40-44

Ezra 1-10
Proverbs 9
Isaiah 40-44

Revelation 5-9

Genisus 15-25
Deuteronomy 7-15

Column 3
Amos 1-4
Hebrews 5-9
II Samuel 7-14

I Peter 1-5
Job 19-20

Psalms 45-49
Daniel 5-12
Revelation 10-15
Proverbs 10

Isaiah 45-49
Matthew 10-14
Jonah 1-4

Genisus 26-35
Matthew 15-20
Job 21-22
Psalms 50-54
Mark 10-16
Proverbs 11
Isaiah 50-54
Luke 10-14
Ec. 5-12
John 10-14

Exodus 15-28
Acts 10-14
Job 23-24

Psalms 55-60
Romans 10-16
Proverbs 12
Isaiah 55-59
1 Cor. 10-16
Solomen 5-8
II Cor. 10-13
Leviticus 15-27
Galatians 1-6
Job 25-26
Psalms 61-64
Ephesians 1-6
Proverbs 13-14

isaiah 60-66
Philippians 1-4

I samuel 15-24
Colossians 1-4

Judges 6-13
I Thess. 1-5

Job 27-28

Psalms 65-70

II Thes. 1-3

Column 4
Proverbs 15-16
Esther 1-10
I Timothy 1-6
Lamentations 1-5
II Timothy 1-4
Deuteronomy 16-26
Titus 1-3

Job 29-30
Psalms 71-75
**Philimon
+Heb.1-4**
Proverbs 17-18
Micah 1-7

James 1-5
Ezekial 15-25
I Peter 1-5
Joshua 6-14
Job 31-32
Psalms 76-80
I John 1-5
Proverbs 19-20
Nahum 1-3
**II +III John +
Jude**
Daniel 5-12
Genisus 36-44
Revelation 16-23
Judges 14-21
Matthew 20-27
Job 33-34
Psalms 81-89
Malachi 1-4
John 15-21
Proverbs 21-22
Zack 1-7
Hosea 5-14
Luke 16-24
Proverbs 23-24
Ruth 1-4
**II +III John +
Jude**

Job 35-36

Psalms 90-104

Acts 15-20
Haggai 1-2
Zack 7-14

John 15-21

Obadiah 1

Joel 1-3

Column 5
Zeph. 1-3
I Samuel 25-31
Galatians 1-6

Job 37-38
Psalms 105-115

Ephesians 1-6
Proverbs 25-26

Nehemiah 1-13
I Kings 1-10

Amos 5-9
Hebrews 10-13
II Samuel 15-24

I Peter 1-5
Job 39-42
Psalms 116-125
I Kings 11-22
Philippians 1-4
I Chronicles 1-15
Proverbs 27-28
Deuteronomy 27-34
Acts 20-28
Jonah 1-4

Habakkuk 1-3
Galatians 1-6
I Cron 16-29

Proverbs 29-31
I Thess. 1-5
Genisus 45-50
Exodus 29-40
Ephesians 1-6
Joshua 15-24
Ezekial 26-48

Additional Reading
II Cron 1-36
Psalms 126-150
Numbers 1-36
II kings 1-25

Jeremiah 1-52

When complete you
have read the entire
Bible and drilled over
and over new
testament
and Corresponding
old

Testament scripture.

There are 1163 chapters in the bible. It takes approx. 4 minutes to read a chapter. See how easy it is to devour God's word, the more you consume the more you desire.

4 Chap. Per day per year	16 minutes	completed Bible once
8 Chap. Per day per year	32 minutes	completed Bible Twice
12 Chap. Per day times per year	48 minutes	completed Bible three
16 Chap per day times per year	64 minutes	completed Bible five
20 Chap per day times per year	80 minutes	completed Bible six
25 Chap per day times per year	100 minutes	completed Bible eight

The amazing part is the more you read, the more you understand and correlate, true understanding, a gift from God. Always take notes because depending on your heights on the slopes of Gods Glorious Green Mountain, you may not always understand what was revealed to you during your study at the higher elevations. This may seem silly or strange, but I have notes in my Bible to this day I cannot correlate.

Thank you John for your guidance, placing my feet on a path to understanding that only through Gods word could ever be achieved. May God always keep your demons at bay and cowering within the shadow of a strong Angel.

My reading reached a fever pitch in the three years of study, finishing 30 chapters daily, every day, and every week with no exception. As I read the many different books I would piece the puzzles together, this book corresponds to that book, this book references items in that book and I began to develop a coordinated schedule. As the reading schedule took shape my understanding of passages and mysteries was profoundly enhanced, things that I had read many times suddenly took new and proper meaning. God was opening my eyes to understanding of his word and more importantly understanding of his doctrine.

In one incredible moment I was angry at what I now knew to be true, the Pentecostal faith had lied to me. For years they had told me God loves you but he will throw you away if you sin. God loves you but you have to be so good everyday or else. God loves you but you must follow all of the religious rules and regulations. How can this be? My bible, with hundreds of marked passages now clearly displays over 300 verses stating salvation and over 100 verses verifying that it is eternal salvation, I will never leave you, I am your father, no man can take you from me. Would a father ever throw away a son? Could I ever throw away my daughter? Now I understand, my beautiful Daughter Alexandria, could she ever do anything that would cause me to throw her away, I would rather die, and Jesus did, he choose the latter.

This I tell you, after a lifetime in church and all I have been taught, I now realize God truly hates religion. Man is the author of religion and the curator of its continued shackling of Gods people, along with some satanic help. Furthermore religion is the cause of 90% of the world's problems, from war to racism you will find the roots buried deep in religion.

Religion and the law served a purpose once, to maintain an elementary relationship with the father for the purpose of preserving the soul for future redemption. When Jesus died for our sins we were immediately spiritually able to access our father directly, without theatrics or earthly intercessors. Effectively ending the need for religion and the intermediate priest once and for all, curiously the end of religion would mean the end of power and control over Gods people. This unfortunately is contrary to basic human fleshly nature and could not be tolerated. Therefore instead of enjoying the freedom from religion Christ has brought, Christians promptly build a brand new version. In fact not only a single religion as the Jewish people had endured, this new version would be multifaceted. Catholic, Methodist, Baptist, Pentecostal, Holiness, Presbyterian, Lutheran, just to name a few, the list is endless.

The apostles shortly after Jesus left began to encounter this very phenomenon. Groups stating I follow the teachings of Paul, I follow the teachings of John, well we follow the teachings of James, the very roots of the groups I have mentioned moments ago. Paul to his credit attempted to stop this church segregation. Writing in his letters Paul tried to focus the different churches on the basic truth of salvation the indisputable core of Christ sacrifice and redemption. The specific points of the new covenant that could not be disputed or twisted into religious dogma, unfortunately he failed.

This new Christian kingdom of religion exists and flourishes under the smiling eyes of its curator, Satan himself. How quickly he forged the nails used to sacrifice our Lord on the cross into shackles to bind his children into slavery and bondage. The ultimate chess game continues, even though the spiritual victory has already been won.

My faith had been shaken to the core, all that men had told me was wrong, perverted and twisted over years of doctrine and personal beliefs. Shaken, but corrected, my God how great thou art, how beautiful and mighty are your ways, I thank you for the revelation of understanding and correction only you could provide.

I now know that you won't throw me away, you are a good Father and you will administer harsh and strict punishment when needed. But as the prodigal son later learned, at the end of the day you will accept me home. I was 33 years old, I had lived a harsh and disturbing lie at the hands of my well meaning Pentecostal brothers my entire life, a lie that had twisted and created things inside of me that are difficult to control, but now I was free. Or was I?

Chapter Nine

Arrogance of Understanding.

Work began on the Church, well a large upper room where a Bible study could be held as a start. My Tract ministry was doing well and I was sending out a religious newsletter monthly to interested individuals. This was truly a season of plenty, my understanding of Gods true nature was complete, I had a good wife, a beautiful daughter and two very nice step children, but most of all I was camped near the summit of the Beautiful, Glorious Green Mountain of God.

During this time there was nothing that could trouble me, is talked openly with Jesus all through out the day and truly received his replies. Most in the form of understanding through my scripture readings and occasionally a near audible voice within my head.

I will never forget an incident that took place during this time. I was driving in traffic and cut off a fellow driver, almost causing an accident. I have never claimed to be a very observant drive, fortunately just very lucky thus far.

The driver was behind me hanging out of his window screaming obscenities and making suggestions of possible vacation destinations for me with his finger. When I came to a stop sign my first reaction was to open the door look him in the face and the following statement came out: "I am so sorry, Jesus love you and God bless you today", the reaction that followed will always be a true blessing to me. The man formerly spouting obscenity sat up straight in his seat and broke into a bright grin and then slightly waved.

The Holy Spirit is always present with a born again Christian, how prevalent his actions within your life is determined on the heights that you have achieved. When you are camped high on the mountain of God, he walks in front of you, easing and smoothing your path and causing the heathen to respect your person. When you camp near the middle he walks beside you and whispers into your ear a subtle correction, warning or advice. But when you camp at the bottom, you walk out ahead of him, though he is always there his shouts of warning and advice can seldom be clearly heard.

On another occasion I believe I heard directly from the father himself concerning a long standing issue within my life. Several years back my forbidden pleasures began to involve cigarettes, after all that's one of the most forbidden of all sins to the Pentecostal. While I was never addicted as most people are, they were a form of sexual stimulation, especially watching my wife smoke them. I had made a promise several years ago to God, never to do it again, in a compromising moment the promise was soon to be broken. My wife and I would occasionally smoke together as a form of for play and sexual stimulation, not often but occasionally.

While being secure in my Lord and understanding that he would never throw me away, especially for a simple carnal pleasure such as smoking, I would become tremendously troubled by the broken promise, it was devastating to me.

<u>Warning: Never make a promise to God! He says so in his word!</u>

I have several preacher friends and had inquired with them in depth about a promise to God. Does God forgive you of your promises that you haven't kept? There answers were all the same, "God forgives everything", if that is true why am I so convicted? Why do I hear the words of my promise played back in my mind on a regular basis? After several years of dealing with this demon I was no closer to a conclusive answer than before.

One afternoon after making a deposit at the bank, I was walking across the parking lot. The loudest voice in my head I have ever heard rang loud and clear, I stopped in amazement. My Father said "My promises are eternal and I expect yours to be also, I will lay the rod to your back until your promise is kept, but as soon as it is satisfied, it will be as though it never was".

How great is the God of heaven and how perfect are his ways that he would care enough for the activities of his children to give personal attention.

My studies continued daily and there was never a day without devouring the word of God. As my understanding increased and my knowledge of God and his mysteries began to surpass the doctrines of my childhood teaching, I began to find fault. A completely unexpected addition to my personality, I began to find minor fault in nearly every sermon or news letter I would read. Major faults of doctrine in others, I could no longer tolerate the ranting of Pentecostal preachers spouting their legalistic doctrines and shackling Gods children to the rigid pews of church politics.

The New Testament is very clear about such fault finding, as the apostles began their ministries there were minor disagreements of doctrine. Paul warned them all to focus on the main topic of salvation, and agree to disagree with the minor stuff. Though these words were in my head also, I could not help but to expound the arrogance of understanding that was developing within my soul.

I remember one occasion, I was listening to a very well known minister from Atlanta, very large ministry on the television. He was doing ok then he made the statement "God never changes his mind". What! I immediately opened my Bible to the story of Hezekiah in Isaiah. God sent the prophet to tell Hezekiah to place his house in order because he was going to die, Hezekiah then cried out to the lord and God Granted him an additional 15 years of life. Yes God changes his mind, read the book preacher! The list of like stories is very long, it was like knives into my ears when I would hear these well meaning preachers making such simple mistakes. As a result I no longer wanted to listen, there were a few I could tolerate with only minor correction. This went on without cease spilling over into my personal relationships with friends and believers. I'm sure I was labeled a "know it all" with good reason, but the truth that was in me was painful to contain. The years of false teachings had to be over written with the truth, immediately!

After repeated warnings to resist the judgmental and intolerant ridicule, spoken directly to me, God, without notice took his word from me. As with everyday over the last three years I would retire to my office and do my reading, that horrible day something came up, In nearly three years nothing had ever trumped my studies, nothing could possibly be more important than my study, this day was missed. To my later amazement the following day I simple forgot, and it would be months before I was allowed to touch the word of God again.

My arrogance of understanding Gods mysteries and doctrines was more than I could manage. And my Father had just laid one of many harsh rods to my person, arrogance and puffed up pride are vanity in the least. To this day I open my Bible and read my written comments next to certain verses and try to imagine how the meaning can be such, it was so clear at one time.

You see the true doctrine of God in its entirety cannot be taught, just as Abraham received the covenant and Moses received the law of God, the understanding of Gods doctrine must be given. A gift from God, just as a father gives an inheritance to a son. Men can teach the basics, often intermixed with man made legalistic doctrines and seldom pure and clear, only a starting point for a climb up the mountain to enlightenment.

Thank you Lord for the knowledge you have instilled within me, I realize the folly of my methods and pray that one day I can be trusted with the understanding of your mysteries once again.

Chapter Ten

The Pure Doctrine

The pure doctrine of Jesus Christ is a powerful and beautiful love story, reaching to the hearts of anyone who will accept its life changing message. In order to understand fully one must place themselves in a position of a loving father. A father loves a child unconditionally, if you truly are his child there is nothing that can change that relationship. Most denominational doctrines state that you must come to Christ, until you ask for salvation you are lost. This is only partially correct! When asked about children dying at a young age these purveyors of doctrine will inform you of an age of understanding, until that age a child is safe in Gods hands. And after the child has reached the age of understanding of who Jesus is and what he has done has come, and the child does not accept. Then the child is lost and on their way to hell.

In order for this doctrine to be correct God must do business in pencil. Placing the names of children into the book of life at birth and erasing them out after the age of understanding. Only to pencil the names back in upon request of salvation. And Christians wonder why so many are skeptical and refuse to believe.

In actuality the bible states quite clearly "I have predestined all for salvation" the Father stated that he knew us before he placed us in the womb. When your spirit leaves heaven to be born into a human body, to make a choice, your name is recorded into the book of life. All doctrines agree that this book of life is Gods master record of all that belong to him. As you enter your mother's body your name is recorded in this book, during your childhood and right up until the age of understanding you are safe within the arms of Jesus.

The fallacy begins at this point, your name is not removed after the age of understanding, it remains in the book of life until the last breath of human life is expelled out of your body. At that moment if you have not made your choice, then and only then will your name be blotted out of the book of life. Revelation chapter three is very clear, at this time I will blot out your name from the book of life. My God is an awesome God! He reigns from heaven on high, and he delights in his children and does not focus on petty and vain human failures. You see he has the ability to regard the truth within your heart and soul, be your intentions pure his grace will cover your transgressions. Be your intentions false chances are you are a hollow vessel, with no true relationship to the father inside your heart and spirit, only possessing a worldly title such as Christian or Catholic. The worldly title will not purchase any reprieve on the Day of Judgment.

Much can be gleaned from the existing remnants of the first Church of Jesus Christ, the Roman Catholic Organization. I refuse to acknowledge its present day existence as anything more than a financial based and corrupted Corporation. All resemblance to the original Church of Jesus Christ has long been replaced by the words and doctrine of men arrogantly claiming to speak for God.

Thank you Lord Jesus that your power and grace reaches even into the most twisted and corrupt fallacies of Satan, finding the hearts of the innocent and true children.

One such example of lost knowledge still existing within the Catholic doctrine, existing in name only as the meaning has long been lost, is conformation. You see when a person comes forward and receives Christ, they are not receiving salvation, that was predestined to them by Gods own words, they are in fact being confirmed into the family of God. The conformation of the choice in which the spirit was specifically sent to earth to make. In doing so salvation is one of the many inheritances, and at their dying breath this confirmation, if genuine, will reflect in their name not being blotted out of the book of life.

Jesus Christ gives every man and women every possible moment of life to simple accept his authority over their lives. Until your last dying breath is expelled you may acknowledge the father as lord of creation. If you fail to do this, then and only then have you committed the one and only unforgivable sin, the choice of all creation, the choice that all must make. The original sin of insurrection you will have committed, a choice freely made through acknowledgement or sadly made thru sustained silence. The choice to follow the creator or the deceiver, this choice can only be made by your spirit through your flesh.

Thank you Jesus that through your grace and sacrifice you give every possible opportunity, to every soul to accept that which was predestined to them at the beginning of creation. Only a lesser God would use a pencil!

The doctrine of Jesus Christ is simple, complete and eternal, if you truly belong to him, that relationship is forever. If you accept him as Lord from the heart and follow his instruction, you do belong to him. My Jesus has the power and desire to keep you within his flock. For he is the good Sheppard and a good Sheppard will lay down his life before the lamb suffers harm.

Christ asks one thing of you as a child of God, follow my instructions and do the best that you can everyday, if you fail today, tomorrow follow my instructions and do the best that you can. I have taken away your transgressions, before you have even preformed them, your sin will never harm me again. Do not believe that you hang me on a cross again and again with your everyday sins, that sacrifice is complete. My Crucifixion was a battle between God and Satan, you were the prize and I won the battle. Take refuge within my victory and peace within my house, for if you belong to me I will tolerate none to molest my children.

My baby girl always says "daddy I love you more than you love me" and I reply "no my love, I love you more than you love me". One day she will understand after she has a family and her daddy is no longer a daily presence in her life. That though she may love her daddy, the love she has for her child will be far greater, but my love for her will never fail or lessen.

I would gladly give my life to preserve my beautiful Alexandria, may God bless her life and command his angels to keep her demons always at bay.

Chapter Eleven

The Crime

God's nature is absolutely pure! When creation decided to rebel against God, imperfection and sin were spoken into existence. Imperfection and sin cannot coexist with God, therefore some rules had to be established. Very strict and rigid rules! Rule number one, the punishment for sin is death, literally to die, flesh and spirit. While the process of physical death needs no explanation, spiritual death for those who do not understand amounts to absolute separation from God.

The soul, originating in heaven, draws its very life energy from God, apparently possessing an unquenchable desire to reunite with its creator. While earthly separation is not complete, as the Holy Spirit feeds the soul, spiritual separation is absolute and devastating to the spirit. Separation from God is as close to absolute death to the immortal soul as possible.

Satan had established his power thru insurrection, rebellion and the violation of the law of God. During the insurrection in heaven a third of the Angels had chosen to rebel against the one true God and pledge allegiance to Lucifer. Later because of his lies and deception Gods children had chosen to disobey their father and obey Satan, thus elevating his stature to that of a substitute god. And by Gods own law all flesh was now defiled with sin because it had chosen to disobey, or to obey Satan. As a result flesh could no longer stand in God's presence as it once did because it was now imperfect and less than pure. Both legally, and by separation from God flesh immediately fell into the realm and kingdom authority of this new anti-god called Satan.

Death being the new law of the land would reign supreme, all would sin and all would die. Gods beautiful creation would lay in the dirt defiled and rotting. Satan by his very nature was tasked by God to carry out this new duty of carnal punishment called death. Along with harvesting flesh Satan would also manage and collect the souls of the world, regardless of their choice.

Destroying the brilliant creation of the father would become a joy to the evil one, perfecting his craft over the millennia with ever more imaginative and painful methods of death. Recording all of the fleshly sins of the different individuals, Satan would use them as a gauge to discern the severity of final punishment. Enslaving the disembodied souls yearning to reunite with the creator, would become Satan's most enjoyable act, some to torture some to taunt, all to be confined.

Satan's newly created kingdom consisted of two provinces, Hell and Paradise; His demons would kill the flesh of the SPIRITUALLY sinful and place the soul of that individual in Hell. Not to be confused with the lake of fire, that comes much later. Hell was simply a place of outer darkness and complete separation from God.

The souls who chose Gods ways and covered their sins with sacrifice were likewise collected up, but then placed in Paradise. Not to be confused with heaven that also comes much later. Paradise was a place of refuge and fellowship, a staging area for Gods people to wait for the time when they would be made pure and holy, a time when they could once again stand sinless in the presence of God.

This Satanic Kingdom would stand for nearly ten thousand years, standing proudly and arrogantly in defiance of Gods authority. Satan boasting of his complete carnal domination over Gods creation, through sin, death and the grave. Claiming victory over the souls confined to paradise by virtue of the law fore which they had broken. The souls captive in Paradise while separate from God by sin, were still protected by God and the promise of salvation yet to come. Satan's authority was thankfully limited to confinement for the inhabitants of Paradise, though he strutted around and taunted Gods people he could not torture them.

A good father even in his wrath can show wisdom and forgiveness, thank you father for your reprieve. Thank you for allowing a "scapegoat" to die in our place.

After the original sin in the Garden of Eden, Adam and Eve by the law of God, should have been put to death. But in his wonderful compassion God immediately made a loophole for his beloved creation. If a man sins he must die OR something must die, "the loophole", a substitute will be acceptable.

Instead God sacrificed an "innocent" animal and used the skin to cover the nakedness of their bodies. This was the first sacrifice and the nakedness that was covered represented the sins that were covered. The sacrificed animal, being lower than man, could only offer a temporary reprieve from death, an imperfect sacrifice.

God's law requires equal justice, eye for an eye, tooth for a tooth, innocent human blood to cover human sin. While there existed no "innocent human blood by virtue of man's very procreation", this limited reprieve would have to suffice. This precedent will become the promise of future salvation and keep the relationship between God and creation alive until a perfect sacrifice can be accomplished. This is the history of the sacrifice, and now I want to explain the sacrificial crime!

The law as God pronounced is "if a man sins the man must die" all of humanity is now sinful being born into sin from the act of procreation by their parents. Side note: God is the creator; man was never intended to procreate. As a result of mans partaking of the fruit of the tree of knowledge his ability to procreate was made known. Therefore through his sin he may now conceive and create life. As a result the human creation, which was designed to live forever, now has an expiration date, all sin and all must die.

The sacrifice of animals covered the spiritual sins but the body pays in a carnal way for it's less than Godly activities. This harsh penalty still applies to all human beings. Before the original sin Adam did not age and his body was always perfect, furthermore he would have never died had he stayed pure and sinless. After his fall from grace his body began to age and wear and eventually would die, this would be the reality for all of creation there after. Except for one man!

Jesus Christ was born of a virgin, he did not enter this world with the same sin nature, he was pure just as Adam was pure in the beginning. But unlike Adam, Jesus went on to lead a pure and sinless life, his body and spirit free from decay and decline and according to Gods law, with out sin he would live forever. So how was he allowed to die? There is the crime! The ultimate crime of all creation, as well as the ultimate deception and most genius chess maneuver God had ever placed forward.

Premeditated Murder! Committed by Satan against Gods son and charged by the very law of God that had been used to separate the Creator from the creation. He had killed an innocent man, murder in God's eyes. Satan only possessed the God given power to kill sinful flesh, sinless flesh by the law of God was still supposed to live forever. A brilliant strategy, there had not been sinless flesh on earth in almost ten thousand years.

Satan had from the time of the garden killed each and every piece of flesh God had ever created, why would he even stop to consider if it were legal to kill Christ? His learned behavior, Satan's obvious complacency with his job would invite the greatest blunder to his strategy and allow God to finally legally pardon all of creation. The perfect, innocent and sinless human sacrifice had finally come forward.

When Satan killed Jesus Christ's body he had committed the crime. Most focus on the sacrifice itself that Christ made of actually being tortured and dying for our sins. But I tell you without the crime the sacrifice would not have been possible. Satan's punishment would be the destruction and removal of his kingdom and power. No longer did death reign supreme, no longer did death separate one from the presence of God. No longer did Satan reign over the domain of souls both good and bad.

Jesus allowed his flesh to be wrongfully killed and then went to Hell and judged Satan for his very own murder. Finding him guilty, Christ removed his power and authority and freed the souls that were under his power. The strict law had now been fulfilled, once and for all, an innocent man, the very Son of God had been illegally killed. A scapegoat, the perfect substitution, not like a lamb or a goat, less than a man, a perfect sinless human man was killed. This perfect sacrifice was allowed to stand in the place for all of creations imperfections. By virtue of Christ's sinless, illegal death, Adams original sin had been spiritually paid in full, blotted out, all of the ramifications of the original sin had been erased, just as if Adam himself had been put to death at the beginning of it all.

God's perfect plan would be a second chance for creation to be pure and holy and to reunite at last with a loving heavenly father, yearning for the presence of his children. The ultimate sacrifice had been given at last, it is done.

The ways of almightily God confound the wise and prove ever so simple in the true essence of his will and desire to reunite with his beloved creation. How clever, how bold and how unselfish, could a greater love than this exist?

Chapter Twelve

The decent

It had been nearly three years in this glorious season of understanding and grace. My demons were shackled, as much as humanly possible I believe, and my life was wonderful. All focus had been placed on achieving my goals and establishing a ministry. While working a full time job, building a church, and reading the word, I was neglecting my family immensely. I was so secure in my situation, my wife was good, she never complained, my sexual needs were basically met, and I was achieving my life long goals. The specter of being damaged goods and not being good enough to full fill my aspirations was completely covered in the grace and forgiveness of Christ's true doctrine.

After the word was taken from me and sometime in the mix of my busy schedule I began to descend the slopes of the Glorious

Green mountain of God. The decent was so gradual that its spiritual effects went unnoticed. My perfect peace, my perfect understanding was slowly being replaced by activities and goal orientated missions. My focus was such that I forgot what had brought me to this point of nearly achieving. And then it was gone! I found myself camped at the bottom of the Glorious Mountain looking up at the rough terrain and trying to image how I could have possibly climbed it.

My wife had been neglected, after the baby she had quit working to raise our child. Our home was very isolated and some twenty miles out in the country. As she was left alone a depression began to affect her day to day activities. Soon our sex life was less than adequate and the waning demons were ever ready to interject their deviant answers to my frustrations. One evening returning home from work I found Marlene sitting on the front steps smoking a cigarette, as I reacted with disgust and anger at this resurrected vice, a part of me was so incredible aroused. My promise concerning this matter would not be long standing.

After several months of sexual denial and constant arousal due to the smoking vise becoming a daily appendage to our lives, the attraction and deviation soon became overpowering. With bewilderment and confusion I could not imagine how I now stood at the bottom of the mountain looking up. And how high the summit appeared, quite unreachable.

For as many of you may have experienced, the climb to the top of Gods Glorious Green Mountain seems to get more difficult each time it's undertaken. I think the general reasoning behind this feeling is based on the fact that with every climb, unless you get higher than the climb before, you feel as though you have not achieved. Along with the religious shackles around ones arms and legs continually reminding you that you are sinful and bad, not worthy, tends to make the climb difficult.

Eventually the decent was complete, my wife requested a divorce and to my amazement I gave no protest. It was as though we both just decided to stop, neither of us even attempted to continue. I love the mother of my child and always will, I wish things could have been different, I wish I would have been the strong man of God I have always aspired to be. Unfortunately my life's lessons have forged a pattern of less than Honorable behavior, and failure has become a way of life.

The demons that surround me and the doctrine of legalist ideas taught so long ago are a never ending, self feeding phenomenon, ever present and waiting to surface. Though I now have complete and absolute faith in my God and his desire and ability to keep me within his fold, the moral failures and accepted heathen pleasures still hang heavy on my heart. These feeling still prevent me from believing I am good enough to draw close to my God.

The only comfort I have within this journey of ups and downs comes from study in the Old Testament. Nearly every patriarch of the Bible rose to incredible heights at various times, and afterwards fell to extreme lows. Sometimes the fall was immediately after a great triumph where God had shown his power in a tremendous way. Thus my conclusion is man does not have the tenacity, wisdom, or strength to sustain any prolonged exposure to the full and complete spirit of the living God. Our basic human nature is corrupt and contrary to the nature of God. All aspects of humanity would have to be subjected and placed under complete control to allow such a prolonged experience.

I once read about two mighty men of God, Enoch the son of Adam, and Elijah, both were in complete control of their humanity, both had reached the peak of Gods Glorious Green Mountain and were able to remain, both were promptly taken from this earth, escaping death to reside in heaven. Of the nearly 12 billion souls that are estimated to have passed through this life only two, aside from Christ, have displayed this incredible discipline and ability. The best that the rest of us can hope to accomplish is to surround ourselves with companions of like understanding. Strengthen each other through companionship, demons seldom show themselves in public, it's the private times that awaken their interests.

Chapter Thirteen

More Than one way to climb a Mountain.

I was 38 years old, my wife had left me some three years earlier, missing my daughter and recently ending a desperate battle for partial custody, my world was bleak. Lonely and profoundly steeped within my self fulfilling acts of deviate less than honorable attempts at pleasure. Fortunately my understanding was complete and I did realize while my father was not happy with me, nor would he be blessing me any time soon I was still safe within his arms.

Charles, my step-father who had for some time worked for me at the same electronics company, while on assignment in Alabama, was involved in an automobile accident. The call came to my desk one Monday morning, Charles has been in an accident, we don't think it is that serious, please bring your mother and come to Alabama.

I can remember driving the six hour trip and praying to God for healing for Charles's wounds. Wondering what would become of my mother if he were to die. Charles and Mom had found a reasonable happiness, he was very passive and didn't mind being dominated and she was domineering and very needy, but the marriage worked and they enjoyed each other.

Upon arriving at the hospital we were devastated to learn that the extent of his injuries were vast. While in surgery the doctor had removed his spleen, inflated his collapsed and bruised lung and attempted to evacuated half of his blood from his abdominal cavity. During consultation the prognoses and expected consequence of the accident was repeated over and over, your father is going to die in the next few hours!

Charles Tucker was not a large man, standing about 5' 8" tall and generally weighing about 170 Lbs. He was a tough man, like steel very strong and stable, always able to endure tasks of physical strength far past men of half his age. I remember when I was a child, the city we lived in was putting in a sewer system to replace the in ground and old septic systems the community had used for decades. Charles and mom didn't have the money to have the contractor dig from the house to the street, which was the home owner's responsibility. Charley began digging one evening after work with a shovel, and some thirty days later had excavated the entire ditch some 125 feet long, starting at three feet deep and ending at seven feet deep. This ditch was a monumental task for an individual with a shovel, and the talk of the community for years to come.

Charley was in critical condition, his spleen had been removed, his lungs were bruised, all of the bones on his left side were broken from collar to leg and the surgeon had cut him from chest to pelvis to explore the extent of his internal injuries. A ventilator kept him breathing and a dialysis machine worked for his kidney's that were malfunctioning. Despite his injuries he was awake the first day and quite conscious, asking with sign language about the were bouts of his wallet and other personal items. As we all spoke what would be our last words to this gentle and beautiful man the doctors induced a narcotic coma.

In desperation men often turn to God for assistance, strength, and salvation, he cares not what circumstance brings one to him, only that you come. In my desperation I turned to God through prayer, prayer for the deliverance of Charles from his afflictions. Charles was a Christian, this has never been in doubt in my mind, while shackled by the legalistic doctrines we had been taught, he was none the less a believing Christian.

Legalistic and binding man made doctrine will not destroy your relationship with Christ, if you believe you will find salvation. Unfortunately it will hamper your ability to understand and grow in his word, placing prejudice ideas and limiting notions of preconceived rights and wrongs ahead of pure truth and what is truly expected of the Christian. In short, Christ without the joy!

In my desperation I would become the intercessor, I would petition Gods royal court on a daily if not hourly basis, I would fast and gain complete control of my nature to insure the task was successful. As my fasting and prayer began I was amazed to realize how fast I was ascending Gods glorious mountain. Within a week I was a daily presence at the entrance to Gods royal court and the closeness to my father was incredible.

My relationship with God had been seriously neglected in the preceding years and the closeness was truly satisfying to my soul. My prayer vigil would last for 6 to ten hours per day, and my fast enduring into the second week of not eating. I felt like a new man completely in control of my flesh, walking side by side with the father and absolutely certain of the healing Charles was going to receive.

Side note, Fasting

Fasting is a necessary part of ones spiritual life and essential component in a close relationship to God. The Flesh desires all that is pleasurable, good or bad pleasure rules the beast. Regardless of the pleasure, food, alcohol, sex, drugs, tobacco, pornography, deviant behavior, the list goes on and on. The flesh if allowed to partake in the "pleasure" will desire more and more, eventually with no limits on its appetite. With each and every pleasure enjoyed by the flesh the spirit is placed in mounting domination by the flesh. Likewise with each pleasure the body is denied the spirit becomes in more control of the flesh. For reasons that need not be explained, the pleasure of food and drink rank at the top of the fleshly craving list.

Several good examples of the battle for dominance that rages inside ones flesh and spirit comes from Jesus Christ's ministry. Each time Jesus raised someone from the dead he would tell the family to immediately give them something to eat. The person's spirit had just come from paradise and a closer presence to God, therefore it was essential to feed the flesh and allow it to dominate the spirit thus creating a desire to stay within the body. Otherwise with no pleasure to hold onto the spirit would immediately wish to return from where it had just come from.

An even more powerful example was the forty days fast in which Jesus endured before confronting Satan in the flesh. Forty days our lord denied the body its pleasure to insure his spirit had complete dominance of all aspects of his flesh. Had he not fasted in this way Christ would have faced Satan just as Adam had faced Satan, with a spirit partially ruled by its flesh. Remember, Jesus Christ faced the evil one not as the son of God, but as the pure creation of God. Presenting himself in this fashion for the purpose of proving Gods creation could and would resist the temptations of the Anti-god. A remake if you would of the tragic drama played out in the Garden of Eden centuries before. Thankfully the newly cast Adam, would prove to be an exceptional leading man and the ultimate hero of the story.

I tell you with complete conviction and personal knowledge, without regular fasting you will not achieve the summit of Gods Glorious Green Mountain. You may climb to reasonable heights but absolute triumph and clear understanding will not come.

I will try to describe the feelings and spiritual control you experience as you begin and continue your fast. The first and second day of the fast are the most difficult. The flesh, your body rebels, hunger pains, headaches, fatigue, and lots of thoughts of "you can't do this". About the third day the flesh tends to relax and accept this spiritual authority being placed over it. Your mind and thoughts become very clear, your body feels wonderful, your energy levels are very high and your desire to serve God swells. This feeling and these general desires only increase as you enter your second and third week of Fasting.

Physically one would think that after a week or two of fasting the body would be fatigued and weak. In actuality about the third day the body begins to burn fat reserves for fuel. Your body stores only the finest energy reserves within your fat cells. This fuel is perfect, unlike the foods you consume which may or may not be exactly what your body needs for fuel at the time. When running on fat reserves the body is using perfect fuel as well as having reduced duties such as digestion and fat storage. This combination allows for incredible energy levels and feelings of perfect fitness. It is at this time when the spirit can and will dominate the flesh completely. It is at this time when the spirit is free to desire the one true pleasure of creation, closeness with the creator!

Consider what I have said concerning the subject of fasting the next time you see a pastor or preacher waddle up to the stage and rest his overstuffed belly on the podium. Take heed as I would wager he is most likely camped near the bottom of the mountain.

His flesh rules his life in most respects and while he may in fact be a good teacher, I doubt his ability to overcome any spiritual strife.

Fasting is difficult to start but extremely rewarding, I challenge all of you to see for yourself and experience this incredible journey. Fasting need not be extreme and last weeks, this you do when the spiritual battles are great. Weekly fasting may amount to skipping certain meals or even days. One should experiment and find the point in which their spirit takes control and try to maintain that fast. This level will be different for each individual, the only similarity between people is that the fast does work and will produce the results I have described.

Back to the subject

Most don't understand Gods regimented and procedural methods that account for the actions and inactions surrounding the everyday lives of mortal men. While Satan is tasked with and wishes the destruction of all flesh, his influence and abilities are closely guarded by the God of Heaven. Essentially there is court held in heaven everyday, God and Satan are both present, Satan makes his demands and pleas, such as, I wish to kill John Smith today for his blatant disregard for your laws. God may reply, do as you wish or in the case of Job, do only certain things. All things good and bad come from God, while his Angels pour out the blessings, his fallen angels carry out the punishment, under strict supervision of course.

While Christ is utterly committed to saving souls. And by virtue of his sacrifice has the ultimate ability to keep them once committed, the flesh must and always will pay for its insurrections and works of less than Godly origin "sins". There are countless examples pasted across the pages of my Bible of payment, by the flesh, for sins with respect to the lives and deaths of the great patriarchs. Even when the sins of the spirit were forgiven the payments for the sins in the world of the flesh was still expected and received.

Be careful how you live your life and conduct your activities. Satan still rules the world of the flesh, you may be a believer and your spirit bound for heaven one day but your flesh will encounter a day of reckoning. The day Satan is allowed to administer punishment for the insurrections and sins of the flesh. Be your fleshly sins few your health may be good and your death may be quick and painless, be your fleshly sins great your punishment in life and death will surely be prolonged and painful.

Men of old knew the correlation between sin and sickness and were aware of the fleshly payment for sin. An example comes from the book of Job. When Job was afflicted during Satan's trial of him, his companions immediately inquired "what sin have you committed?". Additionally in John after healing the cripple Christ instructed him to "sin no more, lest a worse thing come unto thee". There is no way to dispute the fact that the flesh suffers from sin, at the hand of Satan, still to this day.

I tell you with absolute certainty that even today if you could live a sinless life your body would be healthy, you would still experience death as a result of being born into sin, but good health would be yours. Unfortunately that's not possible!, though like my Grandmother some come pretty close and suffer very few infirmities during their lives.

We cannot erase the sins of the flesh; they will always be present like the scares which form with each tear of our skin. Just as your past follows you through life your fleshly sins follow your body to the grave. Thankfully our spirit is only capable of one sin, the unpardonable sin which I spoke about earlier. This sin is covered by Christ's sacrifice and your spirit will rejoin the creator when you die. Payment for this sin has already been paid and no further penalties apply. Of all the things that I now understand, payment for fleshly sins disturbs me more than anything else. My sins are great!

People always ask me "how does God allow a child to have a terrible disease" or "why does God allow good people to get illness"? While the answer is illusive to most it is in actuality quite simple. The flesh pays for its sin with death, sickness and death come hand in hand. The more sinful the flesh the more likely a disease will be placed upon the body. Only God knows the hearts of "good people" they may appear quite "religious" on the outside but the inner man often goes unseen. In the case of children, God says I will curse those who hate me to the forth generation. This is a fleshly curse only! God predestines all souls to return to him on day by choice! Unfortunately you may be born into a family in which a curse of the flesh resides, thus an illness may be endured by a child. God's will? No! Simply a fact of the human condition due to the sin nature, unfortunately the flesh still resides under the law and always will. Christ freed the soul not the flesh. If he had freed the flesh there would be no temptation, no vise, all would be holy and acceptable. The flesh would be perfectly healthy and fit continually with no expiration date.

What he did do was to send the comforter, the Holy Spirit, to assist the soul in dealing with the flesh during its tenure. Once you have made your choice, God's Holy Spirit will aid you in dominating the sin nature of the flesh, until your soul can be freed from the earthly hell of the flesh. If you are strong in the spirit and capable of exceptional domination, you will not suffer much earthly affliction, such as sickness and disease. Unfortunately most enjoy only moments of exceptional spiritual domination of the flesh and open their lives up to the full brunt of the fleshly curse of sickness and disease through sin.

If this indeed seems contrary to your beliefs and teachings please take a moment to question your understanding. Most religion would have you believe God's gift of sacrifice extends to the world of the flesh and your life should be grand, prosperous and rosy. But when poised with the question of "why do good people get sick?" or "why do children have disease?" they tend to just say "oh it's God's will and we were not meant to understand his ways". Interpretation: *"I don't know, my current religious doctrine does not cover that, and I'm really not supposed to deviate from the accepted explanations of most commonly asked questions"*. Seriously, read and devour God's word, all questions can and will be answered. He said if you seek you shall find and when you earnestly ingest his word he guarantees your understanding.

Please understand that while this fleshly sin nature still exists and the penalties are very real, your heavenly Father does wish to bless and keep you as comfortable as possible. All he asks is to draw near to him, climb up the Glorious Green Mountain where you can feel his presence, and he will smooth your path and comfort your way. Let him ease the curse of the flesh and lessen its sting with his sweet Holy Spirit, until the time of complete freedom is achieved and your soul can once again join the creator.

While I do not pretend to know the payment for which Charles was now suffering I have often pondered the thought, for we all know there are no good men! Regardless of his sins he did belong to Jesus, and at the end of the day once payments for less than Honorable works of the flesh was complete, he would be with Christ. As a true believer Charles's going to heaven was quite comforting to me though I still regarded that event at some distant time in the future.

For almost three weeks I had fasted and prayed, my countenance was completely and utterly convinced of his my fathers pending recovery. Believing in his miracle to the point of absolute denial of the negative reports continuing from the doctors. One evening while standing around the hospital bed I directed my family members to join hands and bow their heads. This prayer as with the many others of recent began with worship and praise, but soon a very different string of events began to take place.

My words suddenly took on a different language, a beautiful language of which I had been acquainted modestly over the years. Though I had spoken in tongues on several occasions over my life this time was very different. As I laid my hands on Charles's chest they immediately became tingly and warm, the sensation reaching almost to my shoulders. My muscles were shaking violently and my voice was roaring with heavenly tongues of an angelic character. The prayer ended with my collapse and the astonishment of my family members, no one said a word.

After the evening of the amazing prayer the entire family had peace, my complete peace led to the relaxation of my prayer vigil. After all I had heard directly from God, Charles was going to be alright. Everything was complete, God was sending a miracle and all my prayers were answered.

Charles Tucker died about a week later. In total disbelief I left the Hospital room after disconnecting the hoses and anointing his body with oil. How could this possibly have happened, how can I possibly still have the peace inside of me after what has happened? Peace I did have, the entire family had an amazing, unforeseen peace.

I would realize later that God sent his Holy Spirit not to heal but to bring about peace and healing to a family, not a patient. The absolute and amazing peace that was present at that time of terrible grief was astounding; people seldom understand Gods ways or works and those who pretend to, dabble in arrogant folly. A week later while preaching my Step Fathers funeral I would experience one of the most fulfilling moments of my life, out of death comes joy and satisfaction and a season of strength and focus.

It was with great astonishment and through the death of my step father that I had finally realized the obvious. The long climb up Gods Glorious Green Mountain had suddenly been reduced to a momentary leap. How far away his power normally felt and in an instant it was within my grasp. How inspiring to realize that the formidable climb that seemed to grow longer with each decent was a man made climb. A trail laid with the stones of works and preconceived ideas of the holiness of God. A trail that required physical, spiritual and emotional discipline to traverse. A trail that required exceptional, carnal discipline that the flesh just could not maintain during the climb. A trail that God himself abandoned so many years ago, when he sent his Son to forge a new and shorter pathway to his glory. A trail that while still widely used is not required what so ever.

My God how beautiful and mighty is your name, bending ever so near with your loving touch in times of need and trouble. Smoothing the pathways of those who desire you and paving the way with absolute simplicity.

Prayer

Prayer is a wonderful and powerful tool. When employed correctly prayer can arrange miracles and defeat enemies. God's word has many examples of prayer, but the greatest is the examples of those preparing themselves to go before a King. The punishment for disturbing a king of old could be as high as your life or even your entire family's life, a disruption not taken lightly. One would prepare themselves for the encounter with great detail. As they were allowed to enter the throne room they would immediately offer praise to the king. Example: Oh Great king how wonderful you are, endless is your kingdom and profound are your riches. There are none like you under heaven and surly will never be again, oh great king. As they were

119

praising the king they would bow or prostrate themselves on the floor in front of the monarch. Thus showing absolute subjection and domination by their physical attitude. After much praise and adoration the king would either ask the individual their petition or ask his court officer of the petition. If the exploits of the individual are less than honorable he would be removed from the court often with additional punishment. If the petition is honorable the King will make presents and grant the petitioner his needs or desires. After the petition the individual would immediately praise the king again abundantly as he existed his presence.

Christ has covered our past exploits so we stand no chance of being thrown out of court, but the approach we make to our father has much to do with our petitions being granted. The request must always begin with praise, the praises of Gods people raise like sweet perfume to his nostrils. After much praise ask your father for your needs, or don't, as stated in his word he knows of your needs and he also knows of the joys and desires of your heart. A good Father he is, as he delights in giving to the child the joys of their heart. Regardless of the outcome or the circumstances always leave the thrown room as you came in, praising God.

Chapter Fourteen

In Conclusion

As you travel the roads of life and find your individual pathways, be conscious of the activities surrounding your existence. A spiritual war rages in the shadows of the realm of your soul. While your human body exists in the present, seen world, your soul resides in an attached but transparent world. Both exist in the same body at the same place and at the same time, completely attached, but in different worlds. The heathen man sees only with his eyes, only the activities of his body and the surrounding human situations. Too him all things are scientific and natural, he is the master of his world and the decider of his path, there is non that can or will influence him, so he thinks.

How feeble is the natural human mind, completely unaware of its surroundings arrogant in its conclusions and ignorant of its origins. The born again believer has the ability of extra sensory observation. This gift is not a process of the human mind but a God given ability for the soul or spirit of the individual.

Most Christians camped at the bottom of the mountain never attain the ability to see spiritual activities; their faculties are no further advanced than that of their heathen neighbors. As you climb the slopes of Gods Glorious Green Mountain your spirit will began to be conscious, as your spirit takes control of your flesh, the things of God become prevalent and forthcoming. You begin to distinguish right from wrong, good from evil, and demons from ideology and humanity, thus understanding the surrounding battle that rages for the souls of men.

If a man is confirmed safe within the family of Jesus, why does Satan continue to attack and influence him? I believe my life is an excellent example of why this seemingly futile effort is placed forward. My desires have always been to serve the living God, bring in his sheep, and take his word to a lost world. Through demonic influence constant aggravation and even using so called Godly church doctrine, Satan has diminished my works and abilities. Through evil influence he has managed to hobble and shackle the man of God, where as I should have reached hundreds or thousands I may have reached only a few.

Forgive me my failures Great King, and allow me to remain in your humble service. For there is nothing else in life of any true value!

All men of God have demons assigned to interrupt their activities, diminish their works and confuse their faith. The level of Gods work one undertakes has a direct correlation to the strength, severity and number of the demons currently assign to that individual. I give you the example of Jimmy Swagart, an incredible evangelist, at one time taking the gospel into every corner of this world. His destruction was personally ordered years ago by Satan himself, as his ministry grew, more and stronger demons were assigned to the task of bringing about his demise. As the demons began to become familiar to him, compromises were obviously made. His failure was several years before his fall, his surrounding companions were able to strengthen him and reduce the alone time, preserve his reputation and prolong the great work he was achieving. God would deny Satan's daily petition to destroy him until his mission for God had ended. A premature end as a result of his fleshly sins, but none the less the ultimate goal of Satan's toil, an end to Gods work.

May God always bless you Jimmy; you have climbed the mountain and remained as long as any I know. If the Christian community were a spiritual bunch they would have supported you with prayer and maybe the incredible crusades would still be going on. Unfortunately, out of impossible expectations and delusions of grander about the spiritual strengths of men, we tend to devour our wounded. I feel a special bond with you my brother as I believe we have battled some of the same foes.

My brothers and sisters in life, I can not impart upon you the extreme necessity of not placing extraordinary expectations upon men. All have sinned and will sin again and again and again, all fall short of the glory of god, though they climb and they climb, most find refuge in the mid to lower regions of Gods Glorious Green Mountain.

Your Pastors and Preachers are men, not super human men, men. The all have demons trying to influence their lives, they all make compromises at certain times. They all sin!, hopefully their surrounding support systems will cover and preserve them until they have resumed the climb up the mountain. And as stated earlier if Christians were a spiritual lot they would understand, preserve and support, instead of casting stones.

I once met a good teacher, the greatest they say, he said, "there are no good men, but he also said let the one among you without sin cast the first stone". Is the understanding so difficult? By Gods standards, "there are no go men, no not one" but through grace a good man is one who does as Jesus asks: "Follow my instructions and do the best that you can everyday and tomorrow begin again".

I guess this entire book can be summed up in a single thought, I will do my best to achieve a good explanation of that thought:

While you are doing the best that you can every day, as Jesus asks, that best may not always be to the same level as the day before. In fact there is no established scale for "doing the best that you can" the highs and lows of this statement vary with the individual. The truth of the pure doctrine of Christ is simple "do the best that you can everyday" and if your heart truly belongs to Christ he will apply a handicap to your score and through his grace you will achieve perfection.

Present

The author lives alone in Cottageville South Carolina and spends about ten days per month with his beloved child. While secure in his salvation and completely understanding that the daily battles will have to be fought. He hopes to impart some understanding and support to those who have limited understanding of the true life changing doctrine of Jesus Christ and the spiritual warfare that exists all around. The doctrines of men twist and confuse the children, often rendering long term emotional and spiritual damage. Even after receiving the truth and understanding, the demons within still play a part in ones life, as you attempt to climb Gods Glorious Green Mountain. Remember, Christ is always with you, remain certain of this regardless of the feeble and spiritually destructive teachings of men.

<u>My beloved America How long can you stand?</u>

<u>The Four Seasons of the Great Nation.</u>

On the eve of something wonderful so many years ago, righteous men assembled themselves to stand against tyranny and injustice. With God's guidance these men forged the Great Nation whose foundation they laid entirely on God and biblical principals. This was the great spring awakening of the tiny nation. The seeds were in the fertile soil and the sun was just beginning to shine.

<u>The spring of righteousness.</u>

Springtime was truly good to the nation, the foundation that was laid held strong and secure. The Great Nation began to grow, the unheard of freedom of her shores, cried out to the entire world, and righteousness rang from her pulpits. The citizen's of the nation understood there responsibilities to love their fellow man, respect his property, and to be truthful above all else. All was good that spring, and because they included and feared him, God's blessing's overflowed the Great Nation.

The summer of abundance.

The seeds of the spring truly afforded an abundant harvest, during the summer of the Great Nation. All was well, the nation had grown from shore to shore, her institutions were models to the world, and the land was sending forth missionaries into every corner of the earth. Truly God had established this Great Nation for a higher purpose, and that purpose was so clear, to so many during that wonderful summer.

Blessings of God were complete, and the citizen's of the Great Nation showed their appreciation. In their schools' the bible was the truth. In the nations courts, the Ten Commandments were boldly displayed, a proud government boasted "IN GOD WE TRUST", and righteousness rang from the pulpits of the land, shining a beacon to the inhabitants there of. A summer of abundance, grace and joy. The Great Nation was truly blessed of God.

Autumn, a time of sickness.

As all things do the summer of abundance had come to an end. The change of season came so quietly, that it surprised the Great Nation. Under the guise of enlightenment and human knowledge, autumn had blown its chilly wind on the very foundation on which the Great Nation had been established. The ever-vigilant pulpits that guided the Great Nation for so long, no longer rang with righteousness, they dribbled with tolerance and acceptance, with feeling good above all else. The schools replaced the bible with Darwin's theory of an over active imagination. And the citizen's began to tear down the symbols of the great God who had blessed the nation so. The Great Nation no longer boasted "in God we Trust" instead she proclaimed loudly "I am great and rich and will not see sorrow". As autumn came to a close the Great Nation was still the leader of the world, still powerful, boastful, and yet mortally wounded. A Nation wounded and sick, but too proud to return to the principles of its birth.

<u>The winter of uncertainty.</u>

The cold winds of winter blew hard on the Great Nation, her young men died on foreign shores throughout the world. The institutions that were so beautifully formed lay in ruin. Her matchless constitution compromised to the point of being nullified. The once loving citizen's now fear each other, and respect no one. Her schools had become unsafe for children, and her courts made decisions based on personal beliefs, not law. The Great Nation was now led by a generation raised in the autumn. A lawless godless generation. Men that never knew the great God who had established and blessed the Great Nation. It was now illegal to mention the great god's name within the institution of government. Decisions once made with God's guidance were now made in fear, greed and arrogance, and tolerance for anything was the law of the land. As the founding fathers cried out from their graves for a return to righteousness, the dwindling pulpits of the land were strangely silent. Out   Of   Fear!

The heart of winter

The Great Nation now resides in the heart of winter. All signs of life have faded, and the gloomy clouds of death surround the land. Missionaries from around the world are being sent to the Great Nation, with hopes of saving her inhabitant's. All is not lost! The Great Nation may die, as all nations eventually do, but God's plans for humanity will not die with her. You see America was God's base of operations, from which the word of God went unto all the world. (Just as he said it would do) (Matthew 24:14, Mark 16:15). God's plans are nearly complete and so the Great Nation will be subdued (as all self-centered nations are) (Isaiah 31:1-2). The only answer is to place your trust in God, Because there is a terrible storm on the horizon from which America will not survive.

www.ingramcontent.com/pod-product-compliance
Lightning Source LLC
Chambersburg PA
CBHW071004040426
42443CB00007B/654